AGENDA

Altered Distances

AGENDA

CONTENTS

ESSAYS

POEMS

REVIEWS

Introduction – Patricia McCarthy

This 'Altered distances' issue brought out in the 'new normal' aims to avoid clichés and anything that might be interpreted as 'the hazards of trying to surf the wave of the now' (Michael Laponte, *TLS* Oct 2, 2020).

The voices in these pages come from many different angles, rise above the mundane, and testify to the power of poetry, not only to console and comfort, but also to celebrate man's spirit, and nature's unfailing cycles of renewal.

There is a lot going on to alleviate people's suffering in times of Lockdown, such as Crisis Skylight who, on the phone, on video chats, on email, or via workshops, one-to-one surgeries and general friendship help the homeless. Heathcote Ruthven (grandson of Grey Gowrie, poet and long-time supporter of *Agenda*) sent me a pamphlet he produced of poems by this Crisis group that he teaches. The poems themselves demonstrate the healing power of words inspired into patterns and images of the homeless who have never before written poems. Donations can be made to 'I Am Not Who You Think I Am' www.thenewriverpress.com/2019/10/16/i-am-not-who-you-think-i-am

In a world, now, despite a certain pandemic complacency, where there are many mourners with too many dying of Covid-19, there are also unrelated deaths that are a great loss to the poetry world. *Acumen*'s William Oxley, husband of Patricia, deserves a special mention here. He was a great encourager of independent journals – often wrote life-enhancing notes each time an issue of *Agenda* came out; was a fine wordsmith himself as well as being a philosopher, critic and a real character. Eavan Boland too, whose sudden death was a shock, did a lot for Irish women's poetry and movingly said in a collection a few years back 'I was a voice' which indeed she was and still is and will be, hopefully for ever more. (I personally knew Eavan in her youth – borrowed a pony for her once to ride with me on Killiney beach; I remember she nicked my riding whip that I never used, shared an inspiring Latin teacher with me – at the posh girls' convent sited on Killiney Bay, Co Dublin, where the nuns were mainly titled, enlightened Oxbridge ladies, the exams taken were the English ones – even though Eavan made out she was at a typical merciless, narrow-minded Irish convent – poetic licence I suppose!) And now, of course, at the time of writing this introduction, we are all having to cope with the death of Derek Mahon, one of the finest poets of all time surely and very much a private person who did not go in for publicising himself, so he has been for the most part under-recognised and even under-rated. Read this immaculate poem on his own death:

An Old Theme

I shall die in due course on a day of rain.
Not in the last bed by the exit, please,
with a loud sitcom on the gogglebox
but in an armchair at the twilight hour
reading something favoured by old crocks
(gossip, philosophy, maybe Schopenhauer,
the bit where he says nature doesn't care
about individuals, only about the species).

I shall die soon enough on a cloudy night
not quietly but furious at the outrage,
kicking and screaming as the lights go out.
Never mind; contributing my own calcium
to the world soup with rosemary, sage
and thyme, I will have time to come
to terms with the elemental afterlife –
grimly, of course, if not without relief.

We shall meet again by the shore at high tide
swimming together noisily for a minute
or know each other in a thick cloud
of dust at a bus stop before dispersing –
flecks and specks of that vast entity
'the seminal substance of the universe',
new lives, the range of options infinite.

I was lucky enough to know Derek quite a while ago – met him for
afternoon tea twice in The Shelbourne Hotel in Dublin. He sat there, low in
a chair, wearing dark glasses, always very courteous and urbane. I met him
also once in Paris – of course he was a real European, loved and translated
French poetry… And so he will live on, faithful always to Ireland via Peter
Fallon's Gallery Press which has produced all his collections of poetry.
I saved a quote from Derek recently, praising 'forbidden poetry':

I was talking recently to a very nice young woman who seemed to be
coming from the current literary orthodoxy. She used two phrases of
her students – one was about 'giving them permission to write' and
the other was about 'creating a warm space for them to write'. Now,
poetry written with permission in warm spaces, there's far too much

of that – and that is the voice of community. What interests me is forbidden poetry written by solitaires in the cold, written by solitaires in the open, which is where the human soul really is. That for me is where poetry really is.

This is the poetry *Agenda* applauds.

While on the subject of death – and life – I have specially asked for, and included here, two pieces on Rainer Maria Rilke, precisely because he seems utterly relevant in these troubled, traumatic times. He is so intimate with the reader, that many readers look to him for solace, advice in bereavement or a failed relationship, or for affirmation in times of stress and anxiety. He seems to make the reader his confidant as he questions our mortal existence, the heartbeat in his affirming *Duino Elegies* and *Sonnets* that of the Earth itself. (See *Agenda*'s 'A Reconsideration of Rainer Maria Rilke' double issue, Vol 2, Nos 3-4, Spring 2007).

An amazing find in this issue is the American poet, Peter Weltner and *Agenda* is taking pride here, as is its custom, in promoting this undeservedly neglected poet. I can't resist the temptation of quoting the final passage from one of his collections, *Water's Eye* (with photographs by Galen Garwood), which serves as his own future elemental epitaph and, I am sure, what many of us would like for our own last wishes:

When I die, let me be the sea,
profound, deep, ebb tide or neap,
my fate god-willed,
currents unstilled. Let me be
the sea,

be its brother, the earth my mother,
my father the form of it,
island and storm.
Let me be the sea,
its waters

the daughters of mercy,
be forgiven again and again,
windward or lee. Let me be the sea,
not weary,
but free, no more fear,
spared more being
hurled from year to year.

Let me be the sea, my journey

an endless day, the way home,
atoned, come by the sea to be saved,
redeemed, dreamed of
by a lover
from a long ago world.

And let us not forget: there is a lot of singing in poetry still to be had!

'An Old Theme' by Derek Mahon from *Washing Up* (2020) reproduced by kind permission of the Estate of Derek Mahon and The Gallery Press. www.gallerypress.com

William Bedford

Under the Volcano

Unendowed with wealth or pity,
Little birds with scarlet legs,
Sitting on their speckled eggs,
Eye each flu-infected city.

Altogether elsewhere, vast
Herds of reindeer move across
Miles and miles of golden moss,
Silently and very fast.
                                        W.H. Auden

God's Smile

'Shall a trumpet be blown in the city, and the people not be afraid? Shall there
be evil in a city, and the LORD hath not done it?'
                                        Book of Amos.

I have nothing to offer.
The grim ecstasy of death is GOD's smile,
but which GOD?
And does He know all the secrets?
Is He in charge of the tablets?
I walk on a slagheap of horizons drenched by November rain.
In any kingdom where I governed
the old would be led out into the desert
and left to the music of the sands,
a bullet for despair, or frenzy, or panic,
the unwelcome visitors who attend GOD's hospital.
I am left with the flickering television
and the question which nobody will answer:
I know it is GOD's smile, but which GOD?

Dia de Los Muertos

*'But when I asked how it ended, how he became a refugee, he suddenly stopped.
Then he got up and left.'*
                    Edward Said

You wait in my cells like a femme fatale,
a Dali dream with a clockwork heart,
rehearsing your role as a Hollywood star.
Flutes and horns blow their carnival tune,
and across my room and out of the door,
Scheherazade flies on her magic carpet,
bewitching the waterfall at Mam Tor,
freezing the paths the drought has walked.

I cannot find the words to love you into life.
You write the scenario and refuse to move,
saving your lines for the gravediggers' part.
I could walk to Mam Tor to reshoot your scenes,
but you would stay exactly as you are,
opening the doors to the abattoir,
the leaping midnight of Sacré Coeur,
the aching void of the magician's screen.

Cities of the Plain

'The weather proving cold, and the frost continuing severe, the bills decreased again and the city grew healthy, the danger as good as over.'
Daniel Defoe

Protect us from the summer's heat,
dazzling bright infection
each of us must midnight meet.

Blackbirds call for our attention,
the calculating thrush
and cuckoo's misdirection,

mocking Parliamentary liars.
Bones in the desert dry.
Children burn in Mammon's fires.

I know the scarecrow's funeral cry.
We are born alone,
lonely, rent rooms in which to die.

I know the city streets have grown
a solitary ache,
a wind hot to the human bone.

Yet fury keeps the streets awake,
where the hurt heart must go,
lost in turmoil's darkening opaque.

Protect us from the summer's heat,
dazzling bright perfection
each of us must midnight meet.

Touch of Evil

'Here lives a fortune-teller, and Friar Bacon's brazen-head was to be seen almost in every street, or else the sign of Mother Shipton, or of Merlin's head.'

Daniel Defoe

The stone-eyed gods sell fates
to swell the catacombs,
feed the breeding lesions of the dark
that's never dark or fake enough.

Marlene Dietrich and Orson Welles
sharing hells and dancing hours,
the town a perfect storm
of riot police and lust.

Then Creon's chat-show brawl
bounces grief off city walls
and decimates the air with liquid hate,
his yellow hair a snake dance troll.

But Blondie tells us all,
his billion-dollar curtain call
Yeh-but/No-but/Yeh-but/No-but YEH!!!
exploding every megaphone for miles.

Parasols

'The very Court, which was then gay and luxurious, put on a face of just concern for the public danger.'
                                        Daniel Defoe

The red parasol and the blue parasol
Flick flick their technicolour view
on the mind's inventive screen,
the nervous tick of an eyebrow
rainbowing dreams of paradise:
La Rue Apollinaire et La Rue Seine
where we drank café and talked Camus.
The lecture was not for you.
You wanted a room and action.
But the pigeons in the square
ignored our much ado,
the heat of the frenzied female,
the dazzling display of the cockatoo.
I am grateful for your affection,
but the scenario did not admit affection,
and the blinds in our afternoon room
would not come down,
and you were upset by the girls
on the opposite balcony,
parading their fleshy thighs,
the coarse slap of their laughter.
I am still in love with you,
but a madeleine won't do,
I need photographs and words,
I need words more than photographs.
So until you change your mind,
the red parasol and the blue parasol
will have to do, will have to work their magic,
and the mind's inventive much ado,
that fine Elizabethan fuss about *nothing*.*

Hamlet: 3.2.112: '*a fair thought to lie between maids' legs*'.

13

Letter from Cumbria

'We boast our light; but if we look not wisely on the sun itself, it smites us into darkness.'
John Milton

The sky has dropped. I guess you know.
White dust scatters on forest pine.
A brilliant sunlight scalds the snow.

Will there be loud arcades of time,
flowers to erupt their wild grace,
histories for us? You are mine.

I am yours. I know your face,
your hands, our children's blue eyes…
you not here, I whisper into space.

And daffadillies, Coleridge sighs,
growing quickly beside the lake,
leaping from the mirroring skies –

daffadillies melt and shake,
vibrating in the molten air.
Where poets cherished all they make,

these makars witness our despair,
ghosts waiting for the sun to slow.
Alone, I wonder where you are.

The sky has dropped. I guess you know.
White dust scatters on forest pine.
A brilliant sunlight scalds the snow.

Lazarus

'That the burial of the dead be at most convenient hours, always either before sun-rising or after sun-setting, and that no neighbours nor friends be suffered to accompany the corpse to church.'
Daniel Defoe

I believe I am dead.
When you touch me the arousal is pain
and the bright sunlight hurts my eyes.
I am not ready for this return,
this walk-on we never rehearsed.
Death was lying still beneath the fig trees,
out there in the slow spin of stars,
hearing the rustle of leaves.
I am not ready for this loud miracle.
If I believed in you, I wouldn't mind.
But I don't believe in you.
I believe I am dead,
and the belief colours all I do:
women run screaming when I smile,
old men on bicycles chew their lips,
children in the bazaars weep.
This is what you have done.
This is your miracle.
Yet I am naked. I am harmless.
I bring nothing back. I have nothing to bring.
You are simply bigger than me.
You have all the answers.
So I walk through the rubbled villages,
trailing my bloody bandages,
the yap of wild dogs,
the hysterical sirens of ambulances.
Nobody will believe I am dead,
as if life were miracle enough, this dry rustle of the cicadas.

Martyn Crucefix

Charlie Louth: *Rilke: the Life of the Work* (OUP, 2020)

Rilke has long suffered from two types of criticism. Some, among his enthusiasts, declare his work close to sacred and therefore hardly open to normal practices of critical analysis, at risk of spoiling the 'bloom' of mystery they find in his work. Others, of a more negative inclination, accuse him of an aloof aestheticism, a likely fatal distance from 'real' life. One such was Thomas Mann who can be found, Charlie Louth notes "(rather richly) calling him an 'arch aesthete'". Both viewpoints risk downplaying the craft of Rilke's work (he thought long and hard about poems as artefacts, things consciously and intricately made) but also risk mistaking the particular power of his poetry. *Rilke: the Life of the Work* is comprehensive, erudite, always clear and – most importantly – keeps returning us to the poetry to which Louth enthusiastically responds: "When we read Rilke, the poems do not feel aloof, and they do not feel merely aesthetic in their claims. They press upon us and make us examine ourselves".

Most readers will recognise this as an allusion to the 'Archaic Torso of Apollo' (from *New Poems*) which concludes "You must change your life". Louth says, "It is unusual for Rilke to be so direct, but as I see it a similar spirit animates most if not all of his poems". His new book aims to bridge the gulf between the enthusiastic, non-specialist reader of poetry (Louth translates his foreign language quotations himself) and the German lang/ lit academic or student. The balance between engaging readability and academic thoroughness is finely judged. I particularly enjoy Louth's close reading of the poems, viewed as objectively as possible (Louth declares early on that he has no "overarching thesis"). The kind of closed system of a purely aesthetic art was the poet's abhorrence. In a lecture he gave, early in his career, Rilke is already sure that "'art is only a path, not a destination'. His poems pay particular attention to the processes of change associated with being human; they record such moments of change but also act, in being read and openly experienced, as opportunities in which change in the reading individual might well take place.

For those with faith in literature, Louth articulates an exciting prospect: "to read at all is to pause, is to take your time in times where an anxious haste pervades much of what we do. In some sense it is to live better whether poetry makes anything happen or not". Writing to Thankmar von Münchhausen in 1915, Rilke asks, "What is our job if not, purely and freely, to provide occasions for change?" For Rilke himself, the key change was his meeting with Lou Andreas-Salomé in May 1897. Lou changed his handwriting and his name (from René to Rainer), but it was the confidence and groundedness in the world that she brought to his life that pushed his art "closer to the details of lived experience". Rilke remembered how "the world lost its cloudiness [. . .] I learnt a simplicity, learnt slowly and laboriously how simple everything is, and I gained the maturity to talk of simple things". Lou's influence can be seen in the lecture he gave in Prague in 1898, where he distances himself from Symbolism and aestheticism (the dominant strands of 'modern poetry' at the turn of the century) to argue that the artist must not be "shut out of the great channel of life", but must evoke the constant dialogue between the individual and things, "the strange coincidences between inner and outer out of which experience is made". As Louth says, this is an early statement of the theme which will occupy his whole life.

For Rilke, the successful poem is a space in which the mysteries of things and personal revelation are both explored, or revealed, simultaneously. Louth argues Rilke's view of this was always positive: "there is no unnerving consciousness of the self's arbitrary dependence on chance encounters with the outside world", but equally "no doubt about the existence of an underlying unity to which the poet has access". He was always wary of 'the interpreted world' ('der gedeuteten Welt'), a world shorn of all mystery that most of us inhabit, a world in which language has become dominantly instrumental, "narrowing our vision so that life appears cut and dried without any possibility of the unknown and the unknowable". Louth explains what readers of Rilke value in his work: "poetic language as he understands it is precisely a way of talking that avoids directness and allows the mutability of experience and the mystery of the world to be expressed. It releases rather than limits possibility".

It is in part because the enemy of mystery is language (casually used) that poetry (constructed from language more carefully used) has an advantage over other art forms like painting. There's an irony here, of course, because Rilke learned so much from other workers in the fine arts. Most know the debt he owed to Rodin and Cézanne, but Louth argues Rilke's journey towards the poetics of the *New Poems* began in the period he resided in the artists' community in Germany at Worpswede. A lot of his thinking there concerned images of man and landscape. For the majority of the time, humans and nature live "side-by-side with hardly any knowledge of one another" and it is in the 'as if' of the work of art that they can be brought into a more conscious relation. But because a poem works through time, such a correspondence is acknowledged as "something one traverses and gains knowledge of but cannot hold onto". These are the thoughts that preoccupied Rilke when he moved, in 1902, to Paris, in part to observe Rodin at work.

Louth is right that the poet's development towards a poetry that cultivated the "earthly", the world of "things", was already well under way by this stage. He looked to Rodin's methods for "dependability, concentration and craft" and in a poem like 'The Panther' the fruits of more compactness of diction, a more supple articulation of syntax, a lexis of more precise everyday words and an increased emphasis on the visual, are evident. These are the poems that are held up as examples of 'Kunst-Ding' (art-thing). In August 1903, Rilke wrote to Lou: "The thing is definite, the art-thing must be even more definite; taken out of the realm of chance, removed from every unclarity, relieved of time and given to space'. Louth often draws comparisons between Rilke's work and poets from the English language poetry sphere. Here he compares Hopkins' ideas of 'inscape' and 'instress' as "akin" to Rilke's ideas of object/form and its impact on the observing individual.

Certainly, with Hopkins, Rilke valorises the moment of perception, the process of looking. This, from a letter to Clara Rilke in 1907, is worth quoting at length: "Looking is such a wonderful thing, and we know so little about it; with it, we are turned completely outwards, but precisely when we are most so turned things seem to go on inside us that have been longingly waiting not to be observed, and while, intact and curiously anonymous, they take place inside us, without us, their meaning grows in the object outside... "without ourselves getting anywhere near it, grasping it only very faintly, from a distance, under the sign of a thing that was foreign to us and the next moment is estranged once more". These are little contacts with God, transient though they may be. The way we are to put our conscious self into our gaze and let it stream out of us, so enabling us to 'receive' the object without, recalls the idea of kenosis. Louth's account of it is cool and clear: "the whole process can be thought of as two parabolas intersecting at their tips, the mind going out as the gaze summons the object into its focus". The details of the process may seem mystical, or indeed oddly physical, but the point is that the precise perception and discovery of things is *also* self-discovery, suggesting that the *New Poems* are not objective (as is often said) and not subjective either, but complicatedly both at once.

Louth's chapters seven and eight are both titled 'The Interim', tracing Rilke's life and work from 1914 to 1922. After sketchy drafts of the first and second *Duino Elegies* in 1912, the following 10 years are usually seen as a period of failure and difficulty, of writer's block. Louth argues otherwise. Though Rilke felt it *was* a period of drought (and discussed it as such often in his letters), poems were being written (over one hundred and fifty in 1913/4) and the poet seems to be deliberately marking a break in his writing career to spur himself on to greater experimentation. The interim is filled with reading and much translation work too. It was also his reading of Hölderlin that spurred Rilke on, both the poems and the novel *Hyperion* (1797/99). The *New Poems* are haunted by transience (as is the great 'Requiem' to Paula Modersohn-Becker (1909), but Rilke comes to see poetry's temporal nature is not to be lamented and combated, but is its strength, what "allows it to enter into and elucidate the movement of life".

Years later, the unfolding of the *Duino Elegies* is just this: an initial lamentation at the transience of life, turning towards celebration of that fact. Rilke learned from Hölderlin's abrupt style, his winding, fractured or abbreviated syntax. The poem 'To Hölderlin' (1914) praises him and sets out a programme for Rilke himself:

> To linger, even on what we know best,
> is not for us... Here falling is
> the best we can do. Out of a feeling we've learnt,
> falling onwards into one we divine, further.

Louth argues, "What Rilke apprehends in Hölderlin and works into the form of his poem to him, is movement itself, the poem as a passage 'felt in departures'". The long-nurtured fruits of these lessons in poetic diction, syntax and vision of life are what burst from Rilke years later at Muzot.

Much has been written about the inspired "hurricane of the heart and mind" that resulted in the completion of both the *Duino Elegies* and the *Sonnets to Orpheus* in February 1922. Some may find Louth's one hundred pages on the *Elegies* – a systematic 'going through' each poem in detail – at risk of losing the uplift and dizzying experience that a reader can have with this text, called by its author a "great white sail". But Louth's forensic approach is not a dismantling of the poems, rather "a way of inhabiting them". The poems are about the kind of loss that had always been Rilke's subject: the necessary loss of our necessary preconceptions about the world so that we can (if only passingly) experience its ultimate nature as a wholeness of being. The angels who make brief appearances stand for all that we are not (but might briefly glimpse). The lack of self-consciousness Rilke perceives in animals – their capacity to see the Open ("das Offene") without reflection – provides an alternative way of critiquing the life we live. The acrobats in the fifth poem (the last to be completed) serve to suggest that life itself is "a questionable kind of performance, a contrivance, endlessly failing and having to be begun again".

Once this is felt in the blood and we distance ourselves from a world view in which "theories, the conception of things, have come to dominate over the things themselves", then (as the seventh Elegy proclaims) "Just being here is glorious" ('Hiersein ist herrlich'). Our only chance of preserving such glory is (following Hölderlin) to ensure no particular interpretation of experience becomes "the fixed and solely valid one". So poetry needs to reflect the nature of a life "improvised into a makeshift whole which acknowledges the complexity of life while also showing how it can still be experienced as a rich, meaningful practice". Louth's methodical tracking through the poems is an effective approach because the work itself is "extensive, various, not linear in progression, and often hard to construe, to read it is also to live in it, and the kind of reading required – to be willing to take things on trust, to allow rhythms to inform arguments, to carry unresolved moments, to connect disparate images into promising patterns – is akin to the ways we have of getting through life itself".

Likewise, the Orphic song of the *Sonnets* "comes and goes" and the self-contained, episodic, intricately interconnected form Rilke chooses (the 55 sonnets) yields what is Rilke's greatest work. Here, Louth takes a thematic approach, looking at Poetry and Technology, Sense and the Senses as well as the putative addressee of the *Sonnets*, Vera Oukama Knoop, and the marvellously inventive use Rilke makes of the sonnet form. This works less well because these poems are far more light-footed, less "hard to construe" than the *Elegies*. They require less explication and dance away from the forensic. But Louth knows as much: "The language of the [*Sonnets*] has two particularly striking aspects. One is its allusiveness and elusiveness, a curious looseness and lightness of reference, as if the words have become detached from their normal task of signifying, and approach pure form... The other is the way the language grows out of itself, unfolding genetically and responding to its own promptings, as if it were listening to itself".

Louth completes his grand project with a discussion of the French poems that Rilke turned to after 1922. Many were responses to the Vallais countryside, a place where the restless poet at last felt more rooted. But the lightness and playfulness of the poetry makes it hard to evaluate. Brief poems often aspire to the condition of haiku, or in Louth's words, "almost avoid being writing at all". Philippe Jaccottet in 1970, found in them a delicacy, preciosity, even a kind of soppiness. Many poems have the *Sonnets'* light-footedness and grace, but often without their intensity and reach. Louth's final judgement is accordingly delicate: "There is a definite sense of Rilke taking his foot off the pedal in his last phase, productive though it was, but not as mere relaxation: as a deliberate exploring of unburdened existence". So there is a dwelling in simple things, through simple language which can hardly be begrudged a man approaching his death in December 1926. His last published poem listens to and ventures out with the hunters in the Vallais, envying them their energy and vitality as the dying poet (still fascinated by paradox) describes them as "pressing up close to what's living". This last phrase is a fine formulation for precisely what Rilke tries and succeeds in doing in so many of his poems.

Will Stone

Revisiting Rilke

Photograph of Muzot with inscription sent by Rilke
to the Russian poet, Marina Tsvetaeva in June 1926

Twenty-five years ago I made a journey by car to Switzerland charged with researching the Swiss section of the *Rough Guide to Europe*. The fee was derisory but the prospect of alpine scenery and faded belle époque lakeside hotels who might provide a free room or meal for an enthusiastic write-up appealed. At that time, I was struggling with ME Chronic Fatigue Syndrome and my father had made the characteristically noble and selfless gesture of offering to accompany me and share the driving. Father and son duly set off in my uncle's sturdy red Saab 900 known as 'the fire engine', to our first station in France, the medieval village of Vézelay in Burgundy topped by its famous Romanesque abbey. We stayed in the old Hotel du Lion d'Or at the foot of the village; its herringbone wood floors and comfortable rooms furnished with old antiques instantly beguiled the romantically inclined traveller. I recall the commodious dignified hotel restaurant where we dined that evening, hushed but for the discreet intercourse of crockery and cutlery, the occasional agreeable murmur of gentle laughter and Madame in one corner with her little dog curled at her feet, one eye on the slender waiters who passed discreetly like gentle breezes between linen-clad tables decorated with antique silver teapots. I presumed it had always been so at the Hotel du Lion d'Or and always would be, a place where the carapace of the past had mysteriously never been shed.

The following day travelling southwest we made a stop at Beaune to see the Flemish artist Rogier van de Weyden's monumental polyptych painting 'The Last Judgement' in the Hotel-Dieu, a charitable alms-house, then proceeded to enter the Jura. By the end of the day we crossed the Swiss border and soon were skirting the shores of Lac Léman, on whose shimmering expanse ancient paddle steamers *Vevey*, *Lausanne* or *Montreux* still majestically plied between their parent towns, leaving their diminishing white trails upon the waters like mystical signs. I had foresworn to make a slight detour along the valley of the Rhone into the Canton Valais, a pilgrimage to the last known address of the poet Rainer Maria Rilke (1875-1926) whose work I would later come to translate.

In July 1921, Rilke, seeking to finally clear the creative bottleneck exacerbated by the protracted disturbance of the War, had sought anchorage and the required solitude for renewed creativity in the narrow 13th century tower of Muzot, perched high amidst vineyards and pastures above the quiet provincial town of Sierre. Following a period lodged at the castle of Berg-am-Irchel near Zurich and a last frenzy of engagements and travel throughout Switzerland and the Italian Ticino, Rilke with some trepidation settled into the expressly romantic yet primitive Muzot. Becoming guardian of this Valaisan antique was a humbling experience. Rilke had against the grain to come to terms with roughing it. The ancient walls of the 'stout-hearted' tower felt to the poet 'like donning a suit of armour'. But Rilke had found his place to be, after years of restless European wandering. The poplar at the end of the gardens felt like an exclamation mark he said, an emphatic affirmation.

On empty impeccably-kept roads we ascended the side of the Rhône valley above Sierre until the hallowed tower emerged loftily before us above its serried vines, sculpturally compelling against the intense blue sky. Enclosing the domain were weathered stone walls on which Rilke in rather prim walking attire is seen jauntily perched in a period photograph. Today fences and trellis have been added, carefully woven with roses to reinforce privacy. A little spring gushed out gamely on the other side of the road, leaping and chattering its way across a lush pasture. Fifty metres uphill in a meadow, stood the chapel of St Anne which Rilke coveted and had restored. An elaborate antique lantern from Prague, a gift from his mother, still resides there. Muzot was then as now owned by the same family, the Reinharts, and an elderly descendent of Werner Reinhart, the Swiss merchant philanthropist who purchased the tower for Rilke, is still in residence.

Fifty kilometres up the valley lies the tiny village of Raron, whose dramatically situated churchyard atop an outcrop of rock Rilke had chosen as his resting place, as if midway between earth and heaven. En route we stopped by a florist in Sierre to secure the single white rose I wished to leave at the grave. My father obliged, returning to the car grumbling at the expense of the foil wrapped specimen which he grimly clutched as we sped onwards towards Brig. The church of Raron was reached by a precipitous track from the village, barely wide enough for a horse and cart, let alone a Saab. With horror, I realised I lacked the energy to make a bid for the summit on foot and my long anticipated pilgrimage appeared to be in vain. However, to my father's consternation, I abruptly expressed my intention to drive up the narrow track to the church come what may. Fortunately, no one was about, the village appeared abandoned, and with engine noisily revving we proceeded, ever upwards, somehow squeezing through the narrowest points. A man, alerted by the straining engine, rushed out from a barn somewhere near the top and cried, 'Who the hell do you think you are, Damon Hill?' We had arrived.

The pristine view of the verdant valley floor and majestic train of attendant mountains Rilke had presumed immortal had long since been compromised; new highways, developments and the grey cadaver of a cement works in the distance oppress the eye, but it is still a majestic vista, a fitting eyrie for a visionary. Rilke had first visited the church of Raron to attend a concert, and as he felt the grip of his mysterious illness tighten, Raron emerged as the chosen site, the sacred summit that mourners and admirers alike would have to scale, for he would remain eternally at the same level of the lonely bird of prey suspended over the valley, where the spirit-enabling silence, the mystery of the high alpine pastures seemed to descend just as far as the little church and its enclosure but no further. I placed the foil-wrapped rose before the tombstone, the gesture suddenly seemed inordinately clichéd, but then almost at the same moment eminently justified. Living red roses dutifully wound about their pergolas, their bowed branches echoing the crescent head of the ochre tombstone. All the elements present seemed to be labouring towards a work of art the incumbent would have admired, an ongoing bid for perfection. One had the sensation he had experienced a vision of all this in advance.

Fast forward twenty-five years and I find myself back at the Hotel du Lion d'Or, but without my co-driver. The venerable old inn had been dragged forcibly into the modern age, shrilly declaring its recent upgrades and luxury facilities from panels in the foyer. The old lady had left the building, was no more and so the authentic ambience she had assiduously tended over decades had perished and new owners had simply swept the remains away. In the modernised dining room at breakfast older guests had the oppressed air of citizens long suffering an occupying power as they mournfully scooped at their egg yolks. The bullish young staff speedily, almost roughly entered and exited through the swing door to the kitchen; the lived-in old furnishings had given way to a more uniform bland executive style and the silver teapots were nowhere to be seen.

The next day, having taken a similar route through the Jura, I was once more on the autoroute above Lac Léman, tunneling past Vevey, Montreux, Chillon. I had returned to the Valais for a translator's residence offered by the Fondation Rilke at a Villa in the grounds of the Chateau Mercier, a mile or so from Muzot. On the first free evening I set out to re-acquaint myself with the tower. The vineyard was, as before, swelling now with the 'Chateau Muzot reserve' crop, above the tower looked even more rooted and snug, since the tiny Gingko Biloba tree, a 50th birthday present, which Rilke had planted at one corner was now a billowing giant. Other transformations were less natural and less welcome, for immediately before and beyond Muzot's perimeter a hard-edged new world had intruded, development had risen powerfully upwards, their steel and concrete fronds irresistibly forcing a passage around the natural ancient stone of Muzot. The nearby pastures and meadows which had insulated Rilke and his lonely tower from the world below were now dotted with luxury bungalows of grey concrete and glass or smart whitewashed villas with formal ranks of wallflowers edging immaculate tarmacked drives where gleaming military style SUVs squatted.

Fortunately, the wise Reinhart family had acquired all the land immediately around the tower decades earlier, forming a permanent immediate protective belt, but the once isolated chapel of St Anne is now compromised, hemmed in by one of these invader properties. Most alarmingly of all, electric street lights now grace the lane, destroying the last illusion of rural remoteness. Hard now to imagine that this spick and span lane remained the vague dusty cart track Rilke had known and which had endured unmolested even into the 1970s. As I passed the old entrance to the garden, a series of steps built into the wall barred from the lane by a low wooden gate, something caught my eye. A discarded coke can lay brazenly at the foot of the mossy steps, which Rilke had daily taken. It was the encroaching American materialist 'dummy' culture which Rilke especially abhorred and feared, so how ironic it was that this iconic symbol of that culture had been casually chucked over the fence of his sanctuary a century on, the perpetrator no doubt oblivious to the significance of the spot. Rilke's tower might be unsullied within, but the barbarians were now literally at the gates. Unable to enter, I leant over and with a rusty old vine pole I found lying nearby I spiked the offending can and carefully lifted it out as a surgeon might worthless shrapnel from priceless flesh.

At the entrance to Raron, a bold new sign announced this was now officially 'Rilke Dorf'. A 'Bar Rilke' duly appeared on the left. The narrow bumpy track we had raced up all those years ago was now wider, smooth with new asphalt and edged with smart balustrades. This time I set out on foot. As with the Muzot tower, only the grave and immediate area seemed unchanged, the delicate clusters of red roses on arcing stalks still swayed above their dark green foliage in the sun, casting gentle serpentines of shadow over the famous inscription.

Rose, oh pure contradiction; to be no one's sleep under so many lids.

Rose, oh reiner Widerspruch: Lust, niemandes Schlaf zu sein unter soviel Lidern.

In honour of my father as much as Rilke, I had earlier swiped a red bush rose from the gardens of the Chateau Mercier. I laid it upon the little enclosing wall, the same place as the white twenty-five years earlier. Offering that now wilting bloom no longer felt self-conscious, but a simple act of remembrance for that young man's impassioned earlier visit. On leaving I saw in one of the outbuildings by the church gate another development, a little shop selling postcards and copies of *The Duino Elegies*, *The Sonnets to Orpheus*, *Letters to a Young Poet*, and *The Notebooks of Malte Laurids Brigge*. Because it was so terribly hot, the lady there suggested a drink. The fridge door swung back and I felt the eager breath of coolness rush out to meet me. Out of the icy mist a wall of cans emerged. 'Iced Tea, Sprite or Coke?' she asked, smiling.

Jane Lovell

Three Poems

Linnets

It catches us unaware:
the broken sky blown blue,
the last of the contrails, the last
of our days.
        We watch the light
spilling down cracks in the long hill,
cracks in the long hours.

Dragged from the kindness of sleep,
radio news drowning the strange silence,
we mourn our secret landscapes,
the people we felt we knew
        but will never meet again:
our ghost worlds
and the ghost spring sliding away,
stealing with it our lives.

Each day, we walk the old paths,
try to find our way back.
The elder's in leaf, blackthorn starry
with blossom.
No one speaks but
        there is still song.
Finch and thrush and wren

        and flurries of linnets
           sweeping the sky
untying the breeze with their calls,
questioning the tilt of the earth
        and the shifting hill,
its trees and paths shuddering
with light.

Pinned by Venus

You will not see them.
Prints across the dewy grass
disappear before you rise;

the drift of bees leads your attention
away to the walls,
their beds of lavender and sage.

Words we remember.
There is beauty in love.
It burns.

These trees, we love them.
We trade the long days
for shade or shelter,

tread their shadows in summer,
their mast in winter.

The spirits that dwell within
their bark watch over us.

Sometimes, we leave them,
walk to the castle, look out over
the Weald, its watery
layers of ridge and skyline,

shades of green and mauve
so delicate
they are almost translucent.

There's a comfort in distance,
in ancient things.

Tonight, on the hill, we are pinned
by Venus;

the only thing not moving
in the wave roar of wind and leaves,

the rattle of the corrugated roofs
and gates of the growing grounds,
even the rushing grass,

is us.

What departs

*'What departs at death is 19 grams (= 7/8 ounce) of you
shedding a soft blue light.'*
                    Anne Carson

What departs cannot be measured,
the titanic mass of archived moments:
each tilt or slant an altered view.

Choose just one.
What do you remember?

Something surfacing in rooms
of muted decor: those longings,
the fizz of risk.
            Your thin cotton dress,
sun slicing through the curtains
and the record deck's click and whirr.

.001%.
One thousandth of one percent.
One scene. One frame.

In time you become just a photograph.
One day, they lose your name
and everything that mattered
is gone.

Everything you said or saw or tasted.
Every sound that made you pause.
That sense upon your skin of being.
Of loving.

Perhaps we will unearth each other
on the other side,
our hands still folded around something
we hadn't finished, something unborn.

Feel it now: the soft linen of forgetting
draped across mornings, its faded weave
of birdsong,
the quietest of exchanges.

Belinda Cooke

Caring

We have to hold back
the touch, the embrace
in this strange new time,
also needing to shelter our self.

Other times we couldn't care less –
not in the war zone,
or the Russian mother's
Trans Siberian visit
to a murderous son...

We were not going to be there.
We were not going to
have the last sighting.

And then we were.

And what would I
have done without you? –
she said.

And now I am without you.

I know it's bad for you all,
but I want them just to
put me in a coma and let me go,
release me from this terrible pain,
this cancer pain...

Graveside

We gathered in our sinister garb
like Plath's beekeepers or
villagers in *The Wickerman,*
performing some pagan rite.

We heard the priest's homely Galway voice
and wished we hadn't lost our faith –
while the sun stayed with us
just a little longer...

Your hearse went on its special journey,
two feathered robins on the wreath,
memento to those Whiteknights
walks to Foxhill House... flowers

enough without being too showy –
all of Brian's little touches...
Now I'm heading back
with nothing to care about.

Not the blissful journey down
since you wanted your daughter with you,
this intensity of days like an ecstasy
of months. Now what to go back to?...

Elizabeth Barton

Spring Burial

No Requiem for you,
no grand procession through the town,
no horses draped in ostrich plumes.

They lowered your coffin in the ground
even before your funeral began.
I held my mother's hand.

We stood six feet apart
from the undertaker in her black top hat,
the priest in his violet stole;

the gravediggers wore masks.
Your choir was a ragtag gathering
of sparrows and starlings.

Your altar was the sky,
the light your incense;
your candles were the primroses;

your psalm was the green of hedgerows,
fields, the river's quiet rejoicing.
Love does not come to an end,

my brother read from St. Paul;
the great tits chimed their bells
and a woodpecker drummed.

Your gospel was the naked oak,
its giant arms outspread,
its buds about to break.

A cold wind stirred
among the pines and cypresses.
We went our separate ways

and as we left the cemetery,
a masked man waved,
padlocked the gate.

If Grief were a Bird

it would be a kite
     hovering above our heads –
          pick-flesh, carcass-thief –

unseen but always there,
     circling in ragged disbelief,
          not caring where it's blown,

tossed from street to street,
     tilting and twisting,
          the air its element.

Up there, no comforting,
     no platitudes to soothe,
          no rites to ease the ache,

only the whirling dance of death,
     pain untethered, sighs spiralling.
          It plummets out of nowhere –

tattered wings outspread,
     feathers red-gold, holy –
          sucks breath from our lungs,

feasts on our wounds,
     guts us clean, exposing
          bones shining with loss.

Marek Urbanowicz

Locks

We're all in lockdown.

I'll not be fetlocked
nor docked, my flintlock
I'd prime, cock. lock on.
Where's my foe's loci?

Fingers interlocked
I pray to Loki.
Strange gods, let me look,
my mind's eye unblock.

I unpick my locks,
my knots, snip Time's locks,
watch my dark thoughts flock,
unwind No and Not...

I keep my love's locks
in a gold locket,
find when it's unlocked,
in, through, out I look.

Merryn MacCarthy

A Birthday

After drenching rain, spilt petals on the lawn,
my May birthday arrives. Forty days you are allowed
as a departed soul to stay on earth they say.

Young lavender puts forth shoots on your grave.
Better to watch the diving swifts and swallows
return, like you perhaps, to greet me.

I read your cards from former years, the familiar writing
repeating those treasured words of love still fresh.
You gave me other signs within those early days of grief

lighting up dark nights as if still at home to guard me.
If now you are further off you are somehow closer,
your watchful eye a presence in every room

where I am confined to solitude. Going out
to scent the Spring, wading through lush grass
in healing sun, I spend this day with you.

Vertigo

All the time it's one step forward,
one step back, out of sequence,
out of time. Where is the music
I once had dancing to my own rhythms,
playing by ear each tune?

I could then climb trees
to the top for a dare,
the sky my goal. Or roller skate
heedless down steep slopes.
Now it's sheer fall into panic, pain.

All in the singular now, no duality,
only my diary as partner
in a pas-de-deux through deadlines,
last day to declare, documents
never delivered or lost in the post.

I tend to his grave, just a mound of clay
under lavender now in flower.
But I spin in my anguish. On my return
a light in the hall has come on
as if to comfort me: is he aware?

Hélène Cardona

Binding the Rain

Everything rains
    trees become theatre
  for now it's all piano
I used to run my life away
    ink in the classroom
      nightingale
love that child of me
      wearing blue, standing still
    facing a world full of frisbees
I want to fly the door into yonder courtyard
    river to live with wonder
      she horses me through time
anything can happen
      just like when the wolf smiled
    radiant in the full moon
oceaned his paw to my ear
    we travelled to the jungle
      could smell the notes
    and bind the rain
the jaguar stood
    I heard his thunder
    what are you waiting for?
come with stars to the Amazon
    it wanded my heart
    I wanted to silence forever

Stardust

The night is nebulous
the rouge wearing off
Well you didn't hear it from me
you'll never see her again
don't bring your girlfriend
If it catches you off guard
it will cut you
Absorb it by the glass
drink paper turned liquid
It leaves you numb
a pain so dissonant
laser sharp, burns holes in your memory
Words hunt down to the marrow
nuke out entire galaxies and cemeteries
shatter heartbeats into stardust

Terence Dooley

Furled

The umbrella-stand is empty, where so many
jostled and spoke, where duels were planned:
brollies at dawn, I'll poke out your eye.

The fabric has perished; the last one twirls,
up, and upside-down, collecting rain,
abandoned on the lawn. Are there still,
in the backrooms of bypassed termini, vast

vestibules devoted to the lost and found
bristling with orphaned umbrellas,
the never-to-be-claimed impedimenta
hung from the ceiling like a million bats

indignant or forlorn? Things no-one was fond
of enough to hanker after, to mourn, to remember
their almost inaudible song?

From Orient Afar

The caravan of couriers winds down
the narrowest lane at any time of day.
Bright gems, rare fragrances or gossamer,
or dog food, disinfectant, cereals,
brought to your door, unpacked and put away.
Their monstrous depot sprawls across the fields.
You swipe a lamp, they scurry to the shelves.
Each day is Christmas, these are Santa's elves.
Though spoilt for choice, we mustn't stint ourselves.
They'll even choose for us: bring what you like
as long as you bring something. Oh, curate
my heart's desire. Oh courier, curate.

An ominous omnibus

Sol lucet omnibus
De omnibus dubitandum est

The empty bus, a scarlet ghost, careens
towards the town unblazoned on its sign.
No-one is going there or coming back
three times a day. The driver stares ahead.

He is in service, he is punctual.
The cashless bus, the genuflecting bus,
intones its stops a little mournfully.
It goes unhailed, it answers no request.

No muttering dishevelled passenger
is ostracized. The congregation holds
its breath. There is no standing room
or sitting room. An eerie vacancy,
like a macabre Christmas haunts the roads.
Aboard the bus, the driver stares ahead.

Jessica Mookherjee

The Painter of Modern Life

I visit art galleries inside my television where the Chinese
artist smashes a house down, serves the people crab as a mark
of respect, a dissident joke we don't get in the West. I pretend
to read Baudelaire, my bookshelf – a delight these days, but admit
to who will care, I'm on Facebook and Tiktok. The children, scared,
as I once was, throw charades of brave and fierce shapes.
They don't know what's new, lost or gained. I share
the space, ask the man I'm locked down with, *Back in the day*
when we wore such beautiful clothes, were we stranger then
or just the same? He answers *we no longer exist* and smeared
with bleak extremes of shame, listen to the street clap and wring
their hands. Now the artist, man of the world, man of crowds and a lost
child are pixels made of light and words. The papers aren't printed,
don't say anything anyway. We watch the news every day, stare at death
on the television and I walk for an hour in an ever-growing careless tide.
The bluebells are wilder this year than ever. He's so busy piecing
it together, in America, on YouTube. I try to tell him about bluebells.
I mute meetings in Zoom, pretend to be on important calls. Crowds
are no longer our domain. I think it will blow over, I lie. He can't listen
as I reach for Utopia, a new Jerusalem where no one drinks or smokes.

He says *What about Africa? What about your family in India?*
My aunt sends flowers on WhatsApp, *Show your father*
the Tulsi in our garden. I report back that he doesn't want to see them,
or speak to anyone. My sister says my mother's fallen – so far away.
I tell her to call 111 and that helpline they set up at the council.
WhatsApp blinks in messages: *We went that time to Belur Math,*
in '73 after the war, do you remember? your father met a monk
called Jithen who invited us to eat with him, – my didi, your baby
sister, your parents, my mother. He blessed us because you were
from England, how funny. Ask your father. I send her a picture
of the cherry blossom outside my kitchen. *No, I don't remember.*
Show your father the Tulsi in our garden, in England they call it holy basil.
I want to become a bluebell. The kids on Tiktok make Big Macs,
KFCs, Nando's at home and we watch robots make love on TV.
He's dreamed it all before, he tells me. Perhaps he's Shiva,

who dreams of destruction. I've sent away for an effigy of a Norse god.
I say *little things make all the difference*, we change, a virus changes.
I see tigers in cages on Netflix but they're no longer Tigers.
I paint with graphs, no touch, no mask, no means of escape.

Gill McEvoy

Three Poems

Seeking Escape in a Crossword Puzzle

The first three answers to the clues
were 'abattoir', 'Grim reaper'
and 'inter'.
Random at the time of setting,
but now how sinister

when every day Death snatches more away
and in New York mass graves are dug
to serve the newly dead
while hospitals it seems
are slaughterhouses for the sick.

You cannot get away from it,
this air-borne killing thing
that's shaped just like a world –
each one an agent
of a dreadful Underworld.

A Time of Looking Through Windows

You leave the comfort of the Raeburn,
pass through the hall where chill
grips you in an icy grasp
up to this room where books line every wall
and stand in columns on the rug.
An iron latch, plain wooden door,
a window seat, curtains and cushions
patterned with fruit.

It is not the room but what it might meet
when you draw the curtains back.

You take a blanket from the bed,
snuggle in the window seat to watch,
in the grey and misty summer dawn,
the wood outside where an owl
might squat on a dripping branch, at roost
or, folded in the undergrowth, a deer at rest.
Certainly a fox, at daybreak, trotting home
with nothing in its mouth.

Yellow Iris

A wild flower,
yellow flag,
its stem snapped
by my dog
as he raced past.

In the thin vase
on my windowsill
it has sent up
bud after bud;
each flower
lasts a day.

It's like ourselves,
locked-in, cut-off,
but sending
optimistic gleams
of life into each day,
small rays of hope
that all will soon
be well.

They die at night,
but wake at daybreak,
ready to renew.

Tim O'Leary

The Recluse

Five Extracts

84

They need to make room in the morgue
for all those inhospitable phantoms

as the sun draws us out into dysfunctional
tribes, uncertain, day by day, of our lore,

of how the rituals of gathering and farewell
can survive the creed of dispersal and forgetting.

Or, is it more the not being able to remember
as the milestones are shattered by the train of silence?

Three ladybirds on my door say, this is now,
but the bells I once couldn't hear, send me bony madeleines.

88

Easter Sunday, the streets are void
the sky is a waiting mirror of blues,

the hollow city a new Golgotha,
our flat a temporary tomb

from which we mustn't disappear before
a resurrection we see, or are told to see.

And what of the faith between us,
the dream you said had liberated,

the conversation you said affirmed so much?
Are they just apologetic legends?

89

After all this, what will be the public
testimony of a grateful soul

back from a retreat with a gold-rush greed,
the stockpiling urge in reverse

or a bread and butter need to believe
that, even though the rising has been put down,

things have, indeed, changed utterly?
The tension between entropy and order

will alter as society falters
and the separated mutter their way together again.

91

If you look forward to days not yet lived
as if the ratio of death to life might change,

and everything attendant also change,
the past will still weigh on us, a tax or fine,

and new lines across the sky will mean new lines
in the sand, man against man for the planet's plan.

If that is to cartwheel away in earth and sea,
remember how, through clean air and a winning hush,

the mean flush of the virus brought about reflection,
as if Thallium were being nullified by Prussian Blue.

99

I remember the last time the skies were silent
when a kittle cloud from Iceland threatened to choke

us and we wondered then what things might be like
if such a time became more and more drawn out,

a quivering sword of Damocles above the unruly world –
now we know what danger comes with fortune.

And that was the year mother went with the frost
of February, when we praised a god we didn't believe

in, because it was the god that gave her standing,
because it was the sense of a god that she never lost.

Elizabeth Ridout

Two Metres or More

I saw a butterfly and heard a child laugh in the distance and I cried.
You are here in the many ways you are not.
Each day floating by
as meaningless as a silver balloon.
You had long hair parted in the middle.
The evenings I can see from the cliff's edge of the morning.
Your preferences and unappreciated kindnesses
fall onto my head like the leaves I ignored -
you have never been so far off in the way we talk daily.
Blessings to us now
are the slam of a florist's door, the greeting of an old lady by her
hairdresser,
and the grip of a not to be stranger's fingers
Lack of food, lack of money, lack of sleep
I can use to fuel resistance
but the fact I cannot get to you makes my days yellow.
Through never thinking about it,
I always thought there would be a next time.

We Have These Things

We have these things –
a congratulations card not yet recycled,
a left-behind scarf from a birthday party with the scent of a friend,
a stained receipt of flowers and food for a bluebells picnic,
a coffee cup from a local place which now holds cress seeds,
a virgin train ticket to see one now kindness not to see,
a stub of a cigarette that now seems to mock all the effort,
a basket of primroses I thought were garish but are now precious
because they are from you.
The rhythm of the day has become a split tambourine,
discordant yet unvaried.
Was that the holiness, the transcendent seeing through of nonsense,
when someone gave up a seat for you on the Tube, or picked up your
dropped housekey?

John Robert Lee

from *Intimations*

X

(for Pat Ismond 1944-2006)

'Were your life and work
simply a good translation?' – Derek Walcott *(The Prodigal).*

A translation, Derek, of a kind of odyssey?
Of how I passed and am passing

through this island town
parish of an archipelago nation,

crafting canticles of what I see
metaphors to chant in Kwéyòl melodies

of applauding hordes of surf
cresting the ample bosoms of bays,

of hills smoked blue by early light
and haze of charcoal pits,

of violons, improbable chak-chak benedictions
and chantwelle cantors

with voices like rough-edged, trustworthy clay;
and the familiar grid of the familiar
city, its streets gossiping memories
of our indiscretions,

small victories, voyages
deaths and divorces

our little books in which they find their lovely names;
not forgetting the journeyman dreams:

republic of arts, theatres and galleries
in pleasant parks and gardens,

the public purse a guarantee
for young painters, dancers, actors,

veterans not neglected
exiled to bitterness and debt –

what do they mean, the life and work
50 years of hours, days and weeks

learning from you and other masters
the magic of line-making

the stitching of stanzas strong
to hold the sly wind of shifting

currents of turning image,
to fish exact nouns with nets flung

at sea-deep roots of our languages,
to handle with care temperamental conjugations

of verbs that steer our raft and baggage
with stern resolve to some inlet of temporary refuge?

So what is the odyssey,
who is the meaning of this journey

what signify names of dead lovers
distant friends, dried-up rivers

unknown names of narrow streets
in unfamiliar villages and hamlets,

small-town fame and passing interest
of the world outside, chapbooks of ambitious verse

forgotten columns and reviews
that stirred forgotten controversies –

this life that presses on, always,
under bird song in the mangoes, crickets in the dark hill,

masked isolations, coming storms, tremblor at 3,
add the so-so job, certain faith and safe family,

and, the working of the word
the working of the irrepressible word –

how do they translate?

David Pollard

Lockdown

I sit
my window is a bow window
surrounded by the world
its myriad silences are the dry air
and its monotony of knots and staid mortality
comes licking the ground for corpses
tongue dry on the pavements strewn with blossom.

I sit
dressed as an admiral
waiting for the fleet square rigged for home
below the petrels' love of storms
seeking the air for breath's catastrophe
with wings abroad in circles of despair.

I sit
tired of my nails and lips that are ash
no longer blue and long to go through streets
soak up the strewn guts of the city
rather than sit here a dry root in the dark
my prison face naked against the pain of glass
that sees the world and me reflected in it.

South Foreland Light

The keel lists windward and the wind sighs in the jib.

Beneath the breaking bare and moonlight clouds
I saw the dead of all our days
leap just below the surface
the white underbelly of a fish
rising from the deeps a plummet
of the eye's dark mystery of silence
the knife of night cutting at its flesh
(the smell is in my nostrils yet)
between the words which bound in blind
clutch at their wasting fire
to tell it.

The sounding sea that utters us is but dead water now
horses no longer sound their hoofprints
on the waves
the bell is an occulting bell
that sings close to the shores we walked
and tolls and tolls a stranger's breath
of greetings and farewells
that wasted us into this sullen weather
beyond those earlier summer rivers' lazy leagues
through villages and wheatfields
along the sky's reflections and past harbour lights
and further past the safety of the groyne
past much that wound its way through all the words
that housed our exile into too many tongues
of broken voices
opaque yet all we have
here beyond the currents of past love
and our failed way of telling it
and on
        and on
past the buoy's long westward tolling on the tide.

Outer Owers

We have passed the Outer Owers
one mile south of Selsey
our rotten planks
creaking into the lea of speech by rite of passage
and ritual of green foam
wet eyelids blinded as we pass
above the wracks of earlier sailors
coral bones below the gale.

In this Force 9 the seas are not transparent
leave no wake beyond the keenings
of midnight and relentless ghosts
in banners of salt that sting the tongue
under the eyeless heavens where our lonely
scattered bird plays with infinity.

Here the enormous night has blown us you and I
hither and thither among the wounds of a long life's breathing
beyond the headland on the swell of the two tides
here in a lost bark tossed on the water's shattered moon
the knot will hold us to the reins of the black horses
and the unburied children of our hopes.

D V Cooke

Dry leaves

Dry leaves in a dead time –
The flute heard in the mountains.
Heard a moment only – heard at the time
Of the falling flowers. Yet was there
No joy but suffering? The life
That shrivels. Oh, the world that
Has gone and passed us by – that has crossed
The road and passed on the other side.

And there in a window the statuette
Of the dancer – who with rills
And *ritornellos* performs
A minuet – who any moment
Might fall, but keeps a crown
Of laurels standing by. There are
No dancers in the mountains – only
One who died before summer arrived.

Two photographs: Nathan Wirth from the book *Old-Growth* with poems by Peter Weltner.

W S Milne

The Poetry of Peter Weltner

In his latest collection (*Bird and Tree / In Place*, Marrowstone Press, Seattle, 2020) the American poet Peter Weltner prefaces the volume with a quotation from John Clare's poem 'A Ramble'. This epigraph includes the phrase 'to unseal the hidden cause', and this task I believe Weltner undertakes seriously and successfully as a poet. The theme turns up often in his work, writing of 'a light you cannot find a word for', stating that 'nothing less than paradise suffices', seeking what he calls 'the spirit that dwells deep down in/ things' (the phrase deliberately echoing Gerard Manley Hopkins' 'There lives the dearest freshness deep down things'), suggesting the poet's intention is to go back, to delve into origins and sources. Unlike most contemporary poets Weltner means to mine the light, not the darkness. Nature, grace and insight coalesce for him in 'earth's mute/theology, its promised light of burning ice'. Essence ('an ungraspable purity,/winter white') is what he assays, hoping to tease out the secrets of what Thomas Mann called 'nature's creative dreaming'. It is in this sense that the sea or the sun always provide a back-illumination to his poems, as in the poetry of Robinson Jeffers, another Californian poet:

> The sun is a pale flat
> Disc over hills, whiter than waves' crests until its thick
> Light flames yellow, expelling night into shadows...
> (from 'Easter Morning')

The poem recounts or recalls an experience of profound discovery, 'the surprise of the anticipated gift fully given', light striking from darkness. This is a point I will return to later but for the moment I would like to start with one of the many themes that comprise Weltner's broad and colourful canvas, and that is his celebration of homosexual love.

His homoerotic poems are surely amongst the finest we have had since those of Whitman and Verlaine. He is a master of erotic detail – 'gorging on men's seed' (from the unabashed, unashamedly titled 'Ramrod'), 'Dreams/ give/him to me, lips, hands, prick, calves, all to kiss', 'the ripest olive trees/shine in the sun with a light that pleases/me like the glow of boys' oiled bodies'. He takes a profane and sacred delight in the body :'the body/ reborn, transfigured, made new, transfix-/ed by desire, by a light I have yet to see', 'the ardour that rises in the earthy musk', 'your green eyes/amber-

61

flaked,/dripping hair amber-streaked', 'our bodies strung, bow-taut', 'Oh, erotic man,//lover of all that will not stay'. There is a definite nod towards Walt Whitman in lines such as 'Sing of a boy's boasting as he hangs his jock in a locker', and in 'Stiff/pricks, nipples roused and rosy,/frenzy, desire, whatever it takes/to turn flesh into dance', stanzas gloriously celebrating the male body. At one point we are given a vignette of a 'Threesome' (the title of the poem): 'After the bar closed, three in a double bed/...senses heightened/by their daring...warmer than day/as they swam side by side or dived down deep'. Such a bold, audacious and lovingly sensuous poem does not bespeak a man who has lived by words or by literature alone (he is a retired Professor of Renaissance Literature and Modern American, Irish and British poetry and fiction) but someone who has lived life to the full away from the academy. He gives us wonderful poems on one night stands, episodes of unfaithfulness, break ups, the joys of drinking, crushes, infatuations, fears, premonitions, resentments and rage, but what is perhaps most memorable is his loving eye for the male body, its beauty: 'Sweat. Seed', 'licking sweat like the wine we had spilled on our bodies', 'Balls persimmon sour'. There is a loving relish to the detail summoned. There are elegies for dead lovers and friends who died of AIDS ('familiar ghosts'), memories of loving encounters ('How you kissed his lips, sun-warm and inviting./How your blood quickened. Why you feared nothing', 'Naked boys on beaches, in baths, back rooms', 'Your skin after swimming like oil/on a naked wrestler/in heroic Greece'. He also recalls the early terrors of being 'trapped in a daily dread of being discovered', of forbidden, illegal loves, of trying to conceal his homosexuality, but also the joy and danger of his first sexual encounters:

> Paul. You seventeen, I four years younger...
> You unzip your zipper. I reach
> for your crotch... I, no more mere adorer being fondled by you,
> unaware of the danger desire was putting you in,
> you caged for my being too young, thrown into prison...
>   the sound from the speaker
> muffling my cries, I in the first throes of ecstasy,
> a boy of thirteen freed from the bars of his body,
> and you, Paul, my leopard, my cat with your afterward purr.
>   (from 'First Love in Winston-Salem', 1955)

Here then we have Whitman's 'luscious' sex in 'free swing', its full abundance, Weltner glad to be an apostle of the nineteenth-century laureate of same-sex love, with his own insightful perceptions and ecstasies expressed in his own innovative voice. What I like about Peter Weltner's poetry is that it tells us what it feels like to be a live human being free on earth. It is very refreshing to find such optimism in our current climate of gloom. He is aware of 'the dark' of course, writing that 'I find/ in every/ poem I write I am bidding goodbye'. There are many fine poems on 'the haunting sound/of voices missed', and an especially fine elegy (with a touch of Catullus about it) on his brother, 'you have travelled to a faraway land, my brother'. There are poems of recrimination, 'What it might have been like if we had stayed together', and ones on 'the threnody/poems learn to sing after their poet is dead' – poetry 'a passing reminder/of what once was here'. But transience, mortality, is seen as one thread only in life's pattern, and most of his poems celebrate a joy and delight in life. He doesn't like to dwell on negativities. Life always leaps back with its demands (sometimes its terrors too) in his work. Let's consider for a moment how he achieves this feeling, or experience, technically.

Weltner's voice is very much his own, of that there is no doubt, but it is firmly rooted and ballasted in tradition. The hinterland of the past (stretching back to Greece and Rome) is always there. A sense of enjoyment comes to the reader by hearing half-echoes of Virgil (Aeneas' descent to the Underworld), D. H. Lawrence ('Bavarian Gentians' and 'The Ship of Death') and Wallace Stevens ('Sunday Morning', 'Downward to darkness, on extended wings') for example in the lines 'Mourning/feels like a torchlight/I am carrying, borne/down to darkness by love' (a literary fusion not easily achieved), or of Robert Frost in 'I cross the bridge into woods. I know where I have to go', or Yeats in 'a life less lived than imaginary' and 'Why/does it matter if desire/troubles an old man's body/with its inner fire'. The maturity of the verse springs from the poet's awareness that he is pitching against this very strong tradition, and emerging triumphantly on his own ground, on his own terms, in his own voice. The free method of the Beats and The Black Mountain School of poetry is also there (we can hear Charles Olson's voice, for example, in the phrase 'of pulse/and breath/ and departure' in the poem 'Poetry Is a Kind of Dying') but those fields of experimentation have come to fruition in Weltner's work:

> poetry no more than a passing reminder
> of what once was here, a sign of what the human spirit invents
> that for a while helps us to remember
> the past like conjurors of spells, like magicians
> evoking a lost vision or a longed for story:
> like that morning when the sea's breezes where I lived were as saltily
> sweet as the incense of smoldering rose wood and glory,

I saw, was the sky opening to the sun as a meadow of black-eyed susans
and Wood's blue asters unfurled to its light while a bird soared over a tree.

(from 'Palinode (2)')

There is no form for form's sake here, no content for content's sake, but
a mature blending of the two. Weltner offers us slices of real experience
immersed in the contradictions of life. His writing has a freshness and
precise colour which extends the bounds of poetry. The poetic style he
has forged suits his narrative needs – of first drafts of thoughts, of half-
truths and improvisations that lead nowhere, of dead ends, loose ends,
confusions, discontents, mistakes, 'hope worn thin from our ill-use', of all
the obstructions and impedimenta of life (as well as its joys and triumphs),
the switches and swerves of voice held in check by conscious, intelligible
shapes and structures. This style ensures there is no descent into chaos or
obscurity, the general cast of much contemporary poetry. On moving from
poem to poem the reader feels that they are walking through a classical
colonnade in which each poem is a type of column balancing the harmony
of the others. The poet rewrites the past, his work

> transforming desire
> into immortal things,
> like day's passage
> into sunset's brightest ashes…

Weltner always reminds us that poets should concentrate fully and precisely
on their craft (like a scribe should – see his poem 'A Medieval Manuscript
of Job'), 'thread within thread', missing nothing in 'the intricate fabric' of
the work. He always demonstrates a firm and steady hand in this respect,
especially in his bold and successful deployment of the long line. He is not
frightened of the extended, encompassing Whitmanesque line: 'Early morning
dark is late night's promise for a better tomorrow' (in a lesser hand that might
turn out to be clumsy, suggesting disorder and chaos rather than unity and
order). 'A manic summer storm out of the east breaks through the middle of
the night' is outrageous in its reach and precision. The clear disposition of
these lines, and others, creates a lovely cadence, the poet understanding at all
times that speech and music are bound together, inseparably fused. There is
no falsetto, no hysterical bluster, in the tone. It is always calm and assured.
His lines weave and dance like arabesques. There is never any ornament for
ornament's sake. He is no mere copyist but a master of his own tightly crafted
poems which combine Apollonian order with Dionysian glee:

His naked body like a mirrored light, the glow
off gold, the patina on bronze. An August night is smiling
down upon us with its usual ironies. What two boys dare
by desiring. Eyes that meet in secret and know. So
it is not paradise. Yet call it grace. Call it lives suddenly beginning.

                          (from 'Sometimes There's God So Quickly')

The poet writes with a clear prosody in mind. There's nothing mechanical, arbitrary or artificial about it. As in Whitman, Lawrence and Jeffers' so-called 'free verse' (there is nothing 'loose' about it as Yvor Winters thought) the poet is able to find the right rhythm for the right subject in the right shape, creating a vortex of emotions intellectually held in check. This is a quality not easily achieved.

Weltner writes against the odds, as 'a gull's plaintive cawing challenges the sea'. The poet feels 'the necessity to confront things' to construct 'that which withstands/sorrow's assaults', opposing the world's recalcitrance and obduracy. He only goes to the best models to achieve this, so he can rise to the occasion. A recent contestant such as Geoffrey Hill can be heard, for example, in 'There's an art/to luminosity/that is part/of its darkness', the challenge being that of finding light in a world seemingly growing darker by the day. Weltner succeeds in this by writing at times as a poet of colour (he has worked more than once, for instance, in collaboration with the artist Galen Garwood on a number of projects). He is interested in colour and light in all their aspects, all their spectra, all their nuances, tints and hues: 'pleats of light', 'pink pearl and triton yellow and whelk white of the sea', 'the waves shiny as a satin sash, rosy/white with a touch of yellow', 'a pink gray, yellow white/light adorns the sky', 'the ocean is a gray-tinged blue like cornflowers', 'Sunset is scorched orange, the moon/scarlet after months'. The sea and sun in particular, as I said above, radiate beauty for Weltner, opposing darkness and sterility, in an almost religious manner: 'ever mindful of the sun each morning as it lifts higher', 'how the sun as it rises/sanctifies all things', how 'the sun's light [is] bent toward fall', 'the sun at dawn like a girl filling/a window with light'—how 'the sea's shifting colours', 'an amber moon in a sea-blue sky', can dissipate depression, fighting 'the dark wood of melancholy'. *Bird and Tree / In Place* has a perhaps surprising Christian resolution. The last three poems in the collection comprise an Easter trilogy, and conclude:

Light often tricks the eye, turns fact into mythology.
If all of life is a holy fantasy, then let it be this, this glimpse of you, this clarity.

As these are the very last lines in the volume they echo memorably in the reader's mind. They owe something I think to Dante's *Divine Comedy* which opens at dawn in the season of Easter with a sense of rebirth and hope as the poet goes forward to the sun (emblem or icon of 'the Son'), that 'planet/whose virtue leads men straight on every road', kindling light from darkness. Dante of course is emerging from the melancholy of 'the dark wood', and Weltner's triptych acknowledges too that the world can often be 'hard as marble' and 'empty of images' but still he feels hopeful about the road he travels. In this he is very American – it is the difference between New World optimism and Old World (European) scepticism.

No fine poet works on their own: they have to know what was best in the past and what can be fashioned for themselves. It is no accident that the likes of the major voices I mentioned above appear from time to time on Weltner's palette as types of pentimenti, demonstrating that he is no ingénue, no rookie, when it comes to the craft of verse, that his poetry as he himself tells us is 'spared by measure and syllable'. 'By 'measure' he means span of knowledge and observation, and by 'syllable' he means the music of his lines, which I find to be impeccable. If only more contemporary poets could bear these strictures in mind, poetry might be in a healthier state (it might be free of all the back-scratching and false promotion or specious 'hype' that seems to dominate the world of publishing these days). It is still the case, I find, that a significant number of figures in the poetry world continue to sound like T. S. Eliot, W. H. Auden, Robert Lowell, Sylvia Plath or Philip Larkin without realising it. This is either due to ignorance or a lack of artistic care: in any case it always spoils any striving towards originality.

As a retired professor of a proper discipline Peter Weltner is a learned man who knows how to write, not just someone who *wants* to write (because his juices tell him) without undergoing all the initial hard work and study required (in that, again, he reminds me of Geoffrey Hill). The learning is part of the beauty of the verse. But that in itself is not sufficient, of course, as it would lead to pedantry and superficiality. Weltner thankfully is also a very keen and astute observer of human behaviour (including his own) and that of the rural and urban environments about him, wanting to touch on everything that interests him, rather like John Clare himself. (He is wrong, I believe, to criticise himself when he writes 'I would do well/to think less of myself, love the world more', that tone of selfishness completely missing from his poetry. He is also too harsh on himself when he writes, like Yeats, that 'I long for a life devoted to real/things, not words alone'. His poems are full of life. There is no taint of the academy about them.) It is this combination of learning and insight, of dealing with the world's complexities, that makes him, to my mind, an important poet. He combines the cold observation of intellect with what Pushkin called 'the holy dream of poetry', the ability to catch high thoughts in the clarity and beauty of words.

Music is also important to him. He tells us it comforts him in his old age, in his loneliness and loss of friends, praising 'melodies, chansons, arias like moonlight on taut silk' (in 'Les Chemins de Mélancolie') and 'The lamp-lit solace of melodies' (in 'Listening to Brahms on a Rainy Afternoon in Late Fall'). His love of Bach, Purcell, Handel, Mozart, Schubert, Wagner, Chopin, Delius, Charles Ives and Schumann is profoundly expressed, as is his devotion to opera and lieder in poems of praise to such singers as Kathleen Ferrier, Elizabeth Schwarzkopf, Peter Pears, Janet Baker, Dietrich, Fischer-Dieskau and the American soprano Eileen Farrell. In music, as in poetry, he hears 'a lost world being/restored', 'the peace music makes possible'. In his prose he tells us categorically that 'lyricism in poetry' is 'attentiveness intensified into music'.

This may sound a little too abstract and it is the one thing which Weltner's poetry is not. His most intense interest is in the world itself, in life in its myriad manifestations (as it was for Whitman before him). 'It is right', he says, 'to partake of life's cup', that there should be no succumbing to apathy or lethargy, that in fact emblems or icons often say more than words can, compacting many meanings into a sign. Poetry should celebrate life as 'a feast to be enjoyed' he writes (in his poem 'Lazarus Saying Goodbye'). He is perhaps very American in this, in his keen enthusiasm for living. Emerson said something similar when he praised 'the great and constant fact of Life'. He also said that 'America is a poem in our eyes, its ample geography dazzles the imagination', and Weltner's poetry too acknowledges that fact, incorporating what Whitman calls 'life's richness and variety'. In Europe we are perhaps not accustomed to such exuberance and optimism, but I personally find it very refreshing and uplifting. 'Only my elation assures/ me of the truth' Weltner says. It is in this sense, as I have argued above, that his poetry opposes negativity. At another juncture in his work he states quite clearly that 'Despair is the worst sin', the character of his poems catching the tonality of life at its fullest: 'Of the beloved earth,/of life, precious life', 'Life ensuing, never ending, you, like moonlight/asleep on our bed and I, safe as the stones in the wall where you piled them' in a beautiful love poem for his husband, Atticus, as later also he watches him lovingly cutting 'flowers for a vase', pruning 'thorns off roses' stems'. It is this combined quality of compassion, love and kindness which I admire in Weltner's work as much as anything else.

He has a particular loathing for war as an evil force in history, threatening love and peace, 'the monstrous din/of epic wars and the cries...of dying children', its 'Tongues of fire, ash on burnt lips'. He has written a number of poems on the First and Second World Wars, Vietnam, the war in the Pacific, some poems on Nazism and Fascism ('chaos is the law of nations'), a portrait of Mussolini in 'Salò' ('what monsters men create'), Anzio ('the American/ fleet, a many-headed monster rises, its fiery breath scalding the horizon'), the American Revolution and the American Civil War (with backward glances at poets who have written about the latter, including Melville, Whitman and Tate). Robert Lowell's 'small war on the heels of small war' is constantly in his mind, all those forces which oppose peace and civilisation.

His work is also much concerned with contemporary conflicts and problems, in an age he regards as engulfed and 'enraged by the tyrannies of unreason'. He coruscates the western society of our day for its indulgence in luxury and arrogance, its tendency to no longer 'trust in…vows of innocence' as he terms it. He abhors 'the anarchy, chaos and wilderness' of our day, its decrying of culture ('an unmanned boat drifting at sea'), 'the age of unreason/descending upon us, of an endless winter/in a perpetual dark', of the loss of faith in the efficacy of words: 'A heart/breaks and dies from words distorted…The last stand/of truth has strangeness twisted in it', 'how lies became/normal, natural even, part of the landscape', 'the seasonless world' of the dying (notice how that last adjective concisely, quietly, implies the threat of global warming). Without moralising or asserting, Weltner's poetry resists the post-content, post-intellectual, post-memory culture we seem to be living in today, succeeding through his writing in making us feel human again. He is a believer in human reason and dignity, as well as the bright necessity of passion (Maxine Chernoff rightly praises 'the sanity' of his verse). He hates 'the enemies of the Enlightenment' as he calls them, all those who oppose humanity and justice, those who hijack words for wicked or evil ends – his poems extoll the virtues of the free and beautiful human being in an age of 'ravaged conventions'.

The following themes, although quietly voiced, are all to be found in his collections of poetry: fake news, the squandering of the earth's resources, the cancellation of humanitarian rights, the mocking of opposition and affliction, the stirring up of hate, all those forces across the world which are intent on digging democracy's grave. His work decries the vain bombast and boasting evident everywhere, all those voices which endanger the freedoms of the United States particularly, all those parties which are intent on trampling compassion, kindness, thoughtfulness and tenderness, riding roughshod over justice. His poems are also taken up with climate change and ecological destruction, with droughts, famines, wildfires, hurricanes ('the voice of the Lord roaring the world black to nothing'), towns long since swallowed by the sea, and with what he calls 'the solitary, walled-off place' of the Covid-19 crisis. He grieves 'for lost streams/rivers oceans hills mountains valleys/towns villages cities states', of the survivors of wars, 'the inconsolable' migrants and refugees from those conflicts, the lost children of the world, the victims of revolutions, the homeless 'strung-/out addicts with nowhere but down/to go' (the rhythm enacting the tension and descent at once), 'the horror of no better world elsewhere'. He pleads for charity, succour, refuge:

> Mothers, fathers, love
> your children. Care for them. Laugh or cry
> with them. Gather them in your arms. Move
> beyond the river to the further shore. Lie
> for a while beneath the warmth of morning. Rest
> in a place so unlike your home...

This gives the lie to those critics who think of Weltner only as a poet of old age.

Aging is indeed a concern of his, but it is only one strand in his varied work. He sees himself as 'A heron wading alone and winter-ready', telling us that 'Old age sneaks in', 'My hair's whiter by first light', cursing 'The vermin of time'. Memory 'is a wild bird/in search of a cage' (the 'cage' being the writing of poetry) but it is also a place where things 'get restored/to where they ought to be', allaying 'flesh's weakness, sex's failures, the mute betrayals' of time. He can be angry about age, of course, recording a conversation, '"How old you've grown", you said slinking away, "how sad and bitter you've grown"', or noting that 'the trees are unleaving faster each day,/white hairs grow whiter' (that 'unleaving' again redolent of Hopkins), 'the old neither die/nor live', 'Who does not long to live/forever, like a poem read/down the centuries?' He bemoans the inevitable grumpiness and disillusionment that comes with age, the loss of energy and belief: 'When is it right to quit/believing in life, to say it is no longer worth/the effort, the hurt felt each dawn upon wakening of remaining on earth?', how the old and the 'land of the young/and eternally heartless' always disagree, the old man recalling 'green things', 'searching for some late life meaning'. But as usual he pulls himself up by the bootstraps, finding consolation in 'that good/pine forest, its trees redolent of last things, that sanctity' peace and happiness can bring:

> My body shocks me with new, inexplicable pains every day.
> Friends die or are dying. Old age is a sort of war. The globe
> is collapsing in disarray, too, into chaos from dismay

at men's acts against it. Yet dawn comes, like Joseph, in a robe
of many colours...

Memories of finer days come to him, fond recollections of his parents, of a boyhood playing soldiers, erecting tents on camping holidays (the Thoreau-like ideal of 'swearing to live forever in the woods'), of trying on his mother's clothes, of parties, passions, lusts, a friend's fondness for cats, 'memory playing its magic/ tricks', all 'conjured' in the poet's imagination (William O'Daly has rightly written that Weltner's poems 'clarify imagination'). But memory means more than this to Weltner: it is not merely subjective, it is also an objective force in history, 'a land where I might find peace'. There is a deep and wide sense of tradition in his work. He tells us he wants 'to catch the past', 'to plot historical traces'. In his prose he tells us 'much poetry is a matter of what one finds and borrows from the past', and this is evident in his mining of classical and biblical themes. There are poems on Odysseus, Orestes, Demeter, Persephone, Andromache, Medea, Lazarus, Sophocles and Christ in his collections, demonstrating that culture, the humanities, is something we have to hold fast to. 'A man is the books he reads', he says, 'a library braves/time in a way'. Such thinking holds cynicism in check. Culture, the heritage of humanism, is a place where the surety of love can be found, alongside that of friends and family. Peace and compassion meld in one section of a poem called 'Asyla', where harmony and concord draw together in 'The great/ clarity of love':

> Here, at dawn, hundreds of pelicans, geese,
> gulls rest on the beach at peace
> anticipating flight
> when their massed shadows cloud the ocean.
> A joyous sight,
> compassion like the flocks of them migrating as one...

Art and nature coalesce for Weltner as a force countering the world's evils. This integration, or fusion, is often found in his poems about birds and trees, two of his favourite topics. First birds: 'finches displaying magenta, orange-red,/or golden crowns... Say yes to their music. Be/at peace. A lone towhee might be the emissary/you need to learn of joy' (a 'towhee' is a Californian songbird), something we all experienced during 'Lockdown' surely:

> Migrating pelicans, a few geese,
> plovers, white and gray

gulls feed at the shoreline
on fish the tide's brought in...

Trees next: 'spruce, alder,/aspen gray as afternoon sun', 'the beautiful way
day has of dying time after time in late fall':

The scent of the sea spices the air, pine
cones and dune grass, the taste
of salt pungent in spring breezes, resin-
ous as the stand of long leaves behind him.

At moments like these he brings the Pacific/California coast to life as much
as Robinson Jeffers did in his poetry, 'the coast jagged, sword-tip sharp./To
hear cliffs slowly shattering', 'the lights of the Golden Gate shining/lamp-
like, frosted, subdued in late November clarity', the Pacific's 'worn, jagged,
riptides clashing'.

Such quotations clearly show that Joseph Stroud was right when he said
that Peter Weltner's 'poems look directly at the world'. They also tell a
story (Weltner is also a short story writer and novelist) which enhances his
keen powers of observation, as in this stanza where he sets the scene for a
narrative:

The earth steams. Dark clouds rumble.
Cicadas chirr, flies and bees buzz,
Pond frogs croak, throb, grumble,
Tree frogs whistle. The storm flees east.

This hawk-like power of observation is maintained throughout his work.
The reader glimpses 'A fisherman's boat/sails the sea leaping waves
lithe as a dolphin', 'Scimitar-sharp,/a new moon slips into the sea', 'a
eucalyptus whose bark/peels like sunburnt skin', 'A bull-/dog licking the
scab-dirty/face of a grizzled old man/snoring in a doorway', 'the horizon/
reunited each night with the sea'. Crystalline images such as these abound
in his work: 'twilight burning like ancient fires', 'the light on the horizon/
vanishing like a hawk', 'bees/ silenced by dust and heat', 'morning's
bitter beauty', 'squirrels the rust colours of pine bark', 'the sky with a
light like a forest in flames', 'the sun at its daily/work of searing/the desert
to a blistering white'. At moments in his work there is spark of gnomic,
Blakean wisdom: 'Nightmares are the form/life takes when it burrows
into the dark of caves'. He is undoubtedly a master of the bright, arresting
image, that image which (as in the novels of Larry McMurtry, or the

poetry of George Oppen and Elizabeth Bishop) drives the story forward convincingly:

> It is a muggy morning, shortly after first light,
> mist obscuring Pilot Mountain
> in the distance, a slight
> breeze promising rain.
> In a creek, fishermen
> catch tadpoles in nets for bait,
> the river in the valley teeming
> with pike and bass best caught early...

These are the opening lines of 'Sauratown', the first poem in Part Two of the opening section of *Bird and Tree / In Place*, and they set the right tone, the right mood, for the stories to come. It is a question of establishing the reader's attention, much as a narrative writer might, with bold, swift strokes, encouraging and firing our interest. This Welter does superbly.

To sum up: Peter Weltner is a poet who is a fine painter of words, an intricate, delicate analyst of emotions, and a writer who puts content, intellect and memory back on the map of poetry, undermining sterile maxims and inept clichés. His work reminds me of Walt Whitman's paean: 'Such gliding wonders! Such sights and sounds!' His poetry celebrates nature's riches joyously and energetically, and conveys the finesse and sorrows of lovers without moralising, in a composed tone that always suggests vulnerability, sensitivity and poignancy. His lyrical grace is inimitable, his lines supple, subtle and nuanced, threaded together with a fine technical skill. Although his poems can be political, he is never intent on button-holing the reader, but only in highlighting hypocrisy, humbug and cant wherever he finds it, all this whilst eschewing cynicism and the sardonic sneers we often associate with contemporary poetry, endorsing a latter-day day faith in Whitmanesque democracy. His poetry confirms that poetry can be a 'consoling blessing', and that a writer can stand up to the current contempt for reason and the poisonous ignoring of truth. It is a poetry which opposes brutality and vulgarity. One feels that there is a powerful mind at work in Peter Weltner's work, and the indefinable tenor of that mind is shown in the unique stamp of his voice. His poetry should be better known than it is.

Peter Weltner

Four new poems

Clingmans Dome

Hike again through thickets of underbrush,
foxtail fern, lupine, wood anemone
to a ravine's piles of lumber and scree,
eons-old boulders. Rest there. Don't rush.
Cool off under the shade of hickory,
yellow birch, fir needles blurred by
high country mist. Cross the brook
nimbly, its thick slabs slick with algae.
Soon you'll be near the end. Pause. Look
up. You're close to the summit, journey
over. You detect faint echoes of your feet
when, young, you climbed this same steep
ridge. Try to spot him through the thicket as he whistles
back for you to reach him. Make your peace. Wave your farewells.

After a Painting by Samuel Palmer

Come next year, we'll not meet there
again, each to greet the other,
embracing in the meadow, bare-
boned though we now are, my brother.
The lake reflects the stride of egrets
as they wade, unmolested, in shallows
where an anchored boat's lights rest
like tired hands upon the water
or, splayed wide, a shed flight feather.
We hunt for what's left of a ruined nest,
its sticks and tiny cracked shells. Cows
low near a weathered fence. Egrets' silhouettes
shade the lake, its calm unbroken by undertows
at twilight. A life of suns is setting. The darkening air.

Catawba

A green mountain, low clouds hid-
ing its stooped granite peaks.
Still wet from a late rain
the fir trees' needles, the forest
canopy shone with a red glow
lit by the last of a setting sun.

On my bed, you lay beside
me. Twilight speaks
strangely sometimes. Of pain
maybe. Fireflies, as if obsessed,
flickered outside. It's time to go,
you said, our good day done.

Darkness calls us to darkness. I
should have slept and dreamed
of you instead of watching
the last light out my window
dying after you'd slipped away,
lured by the moon dipping over Catawba.

I never knew, as we lay together, why,
content, happy it seemed,
you let that slip of a moon, seducing
your eye, make you follow
it like some brilliant array of stars
into the dead of night woods of Catawba.

Thomas

Swirling winds tear and scatter petals from a garden
behind a wayside inn, a storm
over low lying hills anxious to unburden
itself of its rain, to form
itself into thin white clouds again, peacefully drifting
through skies, no more maddened
by the lightning that gashes the land, the heaving
thunder it is fated to carry inside it, saddened
to have to frighten you: like a man showing his wounds, offering
for you to touch them, still oozing, not fully healed,
wanting to let you feel how his pain
is not who he is, hoping if he revealed
them to you you'd know it is not sorrow
alone suffering brings, nor is it spring yet either, come tomorrow.

Tony Roberts

Robert Hass: a Voice in My Ear

i

In the introduction to his translation of Horace's Epistles, David Ferry wrote, 'It's the voice that's the life of these poems'. He characterized it, then added, 'The voice is an invention, of course, or a playing field of inventions, but it gives the illusion of speaking to us as we hear it with a startlingly familiar immediacy.' Robert Hass also has an endearing immediacy. If I were to characterize his voice – the recognisable personality in his writing – as Ferry does Horace's, I would call it welcoming, conversational, observant, good-humoured and ethical.

Of course with writers who lean toward the autobiographical it is well to remember that the poetic identity is flexible. In a famous interview for *The Paris Review*, in 1961, Robert Lowell spoke of his autobiographical masterpiece *Life Studies* (1959). Lowell reminded his interviewer that 'There's a good deal of tinkering with fact. You leave out a lot, and emphasize this and not that. Your actual experience is a complete flux.' He added, 'the reader was to believe he was getting the *real* Robert Lowell.'

As a teacher – and that is the stance in his poetry and prose – Hass avoids trying to sound definitive, omniscient, standing openly with his audience. In an essay 'On Teaching Poetry' he explained, 'teaching poetry for me has been mostly about reflecting on what makes particular poems come alive to me and trying to convey that experience to others'.

In his own interview in *The Paris Review* (2020), there is a photograph of Hass with the haircut of the time (California 1980) and a wine glass in one hand. He is responding to the photographer with his tongue out. It is a common pose, a humorous 'Get out of here' we are familiar with in our own lives. What struck me (lightly) about it was that in his poetry as in his prose, Hass is the last person to pull a face at his audience. 'Which writer does?' you may ask. Well, few, I suppose. But my point is that Hass's voice is unusually trustworthy. Even his anger – and there is anger on humanitarian/ ecological grounds – is controlled. It is the voice that has kept me reading Hass this past twenty-something years.

And yet I didn't want to begin my appreciation this way. I wanted to write 'I want to say some things against Robert Hass's poems, which I love.' I wanted to say that, not because it's true – the part about saying things *against* is not true... except if I pointed to occasional moments I find too

77

laid-back or ingenuous – but because that is a line he wrote many years ago in a revealing essay on the remarkable James Wright. I wanted to begin this way to illustrate how Hass can put a line in your thoughts for twenty years in prose as well as he can in poems like his well-known 'Meditation at Lagunitas' ('All the new thinking is about loss. / In this it resembles all the old thinking.')

I have puzzled over that poem since I discovered it in my favourite American anthology, J.D. McClatchy's *The Vintage Book of Contemporary American Poetry*, which I bought in Virginia in August 1992 (and from which I also picked-up on Wright, Dave Smith, Donald Justice, Galway Kinnell and others). I have puzzled over Hass as he has puzzled over Wallace Stevens and I have sought no final opinion because, as he said elsewhere in the prose collection that housed his Wright essay, *Twentieth Century Pleasures* (1984), when poetry gets into the blood it becomes 'difficult to conduct an argument about its value' because 'it becomes autobiography there'. (I subsequently took *Poetry in the Blood* as a title for an anthology I edited for Shoestring Press in 2014.)

ii

I hear the same Hassian voice in both the poetry and the prose, but I begin with the prose to honour the line about Wright. So, what are the features of Hass's voice that have so appealed to me? Firstly it is his enthusiasm, delivered in that relaxed American idiom (about which William Carlos Williams once wrote, 'The future American poetry has to arise from speech – American, not English... from what we *hear* in America'). With that goes a fondness for anecdote and a willingness to be involved. Here is an example from *Now & Then: The Poet's Choice Columns, 1997–2000* (2007), a nationally syndicated column. Of his interest in Wallace Stevens he writes:

> In Hartford this autumn, a friend drove me by the offices of the
> Hartford Insurance Company and the house where Stevens lived. I
> had read that he walked to work, and, taking what seemed the shortest
> way, I tried to walk his walk to work.

Addressing a poetry audience, in *Twentieth Century Pleasures*, we find him in similarly informal mood: Here is Hass discussing Rilke's 'Sometimes a Man Stands Up During Supper' and its translation by Robert Bly: 'the poem had a feeling of being too neat, too pat, which disappears, I think, in the English translation, which is a marvelous poem, but one made from the unmetred, unrhymed cadences of a poetic revolution that hadn't occurred yet.'

Here is Hass from *What Light Can Do* (2012), his second collection of essays. The tone is again conversational, the critical insights accessible and illuminating. Quoting Stevens 'Of Mere Being' ('The palm at the end of the mind, / Beyond the last thought, rises / In the bronze décor') he adds: 'And then he changed "distance" to "décor". It's as if he had, in one stroke, made the philosophical leap from Romanticism to postmodernism, from the idea of the meaning of the world as attainable but just out of reach to the idea of the world as a stage set, a set of fictions.'

In 1994 Hass published *The Essential Haiku: Versions of Bashō, Buson, and Issa*. His Japanese studies have contributed to his calmness, sensitivity to nature and to his novel imagery. Here is an example of the last from *A Little Book on Form: An Exploration into the Formal Imagination of Poetry* (2017) – actually a big book – intended for young poets who were taking an intensive course: 'At the simplest level the blank verse stanza works like a paragraph does in prose. But it can also mime the rivery movement of the mind in quietly spectacular ways, as in "Tintern Abbey," or the pulses of thought as it does in "Frost at Midnight".'

iii

Hass's poetry and prose inform each other. In a 2016 interview with Viorica Patea he described himself as operating 'like many writers of my generation on a kind of cusp between late modernism and postmodernism.' His roots, he acknowledged, were in the romantic poetry of Whitman and Wordsworth, which may have also contributed to his longer lines and fondness for plain speaking – along with the Japanese tradition ('Somebody asked Buson if there was a trick to poetry, maybe to haiku, and he said, Yes, learn how to be simple without being vulgar').

Hass's first collection, *Field Guide* (1973) revealed the ecological sensitivity in his work, his delight in naming and friendship, and in the activities of hands. He is often engaged with domestic details which provide the serendipities.

In 'Adhesive: For Earlene', a poem for his first wife, Hass describes the simple pleasures of marriage and a cheerful poverty where they skip lunch to buy tickets for 'Les Enfants de Paradis'. In 'Fall' they are uncertainly gathering mushrooms 'which smelled of camphor and the fog-soaked earth':

Friends called our aromatic fungi
liebestoads and only ate the ones
that we most certainly survived.

79

There is a rich awareness of the gift of living, like discovering trash nocturnal creatures have scattered:

> A thaw turned up
> the lobster shells from Christmas Eve.
> They rotted in the yard
> and standing in the muddy field I caught,
> as if across great distances,
> a faint rank fragrance of the sea.
> ('In Weather')

Simple pleasures are uppermost, but there is a hint of childhood distress ('House') and recognition of historical and contemporary abuses. In 'Palo Alto: The Marshes', we see a tanker from the Dow Chemical Company which is manufacturing napalm locally.

Hass now reckons, 'In *Field Guide* naming the world more or less committed me to the concrete, which tended to be rendered in staccato and short-breathed language.' These, he says, are the poems of a young man who had learnt from Lowell's early poetry of New England that poems could resonate from the regional.

In *Praise*, his 1979 collection, the approach is more meditative, more metaphysical and the lines become longer. Take the opening poem 'Heroic Simile', which distils Hass's thoughts on the limitations of the imagination and the need to recognise 'the silence of separate fidelities'. Or 'Meditation at Lagunitas', the poem which leads away from talk with all its obstructiveness, toward the simple rituals of loving, making bread, and sounding the language. While these poems suggest the limits of empathy, they also recognise the richness of plurality.

Human Wishes appeared in 1989. Hass had been experimenting with prose and some of these poems are in paragraph form. 'Vintage' opens with 'They had agreed, walking into the delicatessen on Sixth Avenue, that / their friends' affairs were focused and saddened by massive projections'. Personal histories are the subject of a number of poems and anecdotes. Being Hass, there are also paeans to the community and to the ecology of the Sierras. The rhythms of life and casual beauty flow into 'Late Spring':

> and after swimming, white wine; and the sharing of stories before din-
> ner is prolonged because the relations of the children in the neighbor-
> hood have acquired village intensity and the stories take longer telling.

Strangers are as comfortably included in Hass's world as friends are. The 'Museum' presents a couple with a sleeping baby sharing the newspaper and Hass observing, having 'fallen in love with this equitable arrangement'. There are couples in 'Quartet' whose inner life he imagines and anecdotes from a friend about himself and the former Vice President, about a duck-hunting judge, a composer who had had a double mastectomy (also the subject of a short story by Richard Ford) and in 'On Squaw Peak' a gesture at that inclusiveness:

> It was the abundance
> the world gives, the more-than-you-bargained-for
> surprise of it, waves breaking,
> the sudden fragrance of the mimulus at creekside
> sharpened by the summer dust.

From 1995 to 1997, Hass served as the United States poet laureate. In that time he published *Sun Under Wood* (1996), a more autobiographical collection, revealing the difficulties rather than the simple pleasures in his own life. In 'My Mother's Nipples' he writes, 'In grammar school, whenever she'd start to drink, / she panicked and made amends by baking chocolate cake'. And in 'Regalia for a Black Hat Dancer' she is living the last of her life breathlessly in a hotel room, while Hass's brother is 'in the psych ward / at San Francisco General' coming down from 'crack'.

The same poem has reference to the end of Hass's marriage: to the 'two emptinesses: one made of pain and desire / and one made of vacancy'. But if sadness and cruelty seem 'infinite' and pain hollows out its victim, there is also the possibility of experiencing a revitalising new love (the poet's second wife, Brenda Hillman). Life has taught him the lesson: 'Private pain is easy, in a way. It doesn't go away, / but you can teach yourself to see its size. Invent a ritual.'

To that end, perhaps, the idea of singing first appears in 'Faint Music':

> I had the idea that the world's so full of pain
> it must sometimes make a kind of singing.
> And that the sequence helps, as much as order helps –
> First an ego, and then pain, and then the singing.

And despite the pressures and pains in the course of it, 'Interrupted Meditation' ends: 'I'm a little ashamed that I want to end this poem / singing, but I want to end this poem singing'.

Time and Materials: Poems 1997–2005 (2007) won both the National Book Award and the Pulitzer Prize. When I wrote of it on its appearance I stressed the vitality and I still see that. However, on re-reading now, the *Weltschmerz* is uppermost. Hass is not a consolatory writer, or at least one side of him is not. One side is that observer – of that Japanese tradition – and this time, re-reading the darker poems, it came through most forcefully. In 'Winged and Acid Dark' he writes of abuses: 'We pass these things on, / probably, because we are what we can imagine.' We wonder at what pain teaches us in 'The World as Will and Representation', which ends:

> My mother at the kitchen table gagged and drank,
> Drank and gagged. We get our first moral idea
> About the world – about justice and power,
> Gender and the order of things – from somewhere.

Then there are the grim statistical poems, 'A Poem' ('The nations of the / world could stop setting an example for suicide bombers.'), 'Bush's War' ('It's not just / The violence, it's a taste for power / That amounts to contempt for the body') and in 'Ezra Pound's Proposition' we follow the economic process by which a girl-child is forced to turn prostitute.

After *The Apple Trees at Olema: New and Selected Poems* (2010), which included a poem on his brother's death and another on leaving his failed marriage, *Summer Snow* appeared this year. It is a particularly fine collection, gathered over the past ten years, a collection which covers Hass's lifelong preoccupations. Old heroes reappear: Milosz (a friend and constant source of inspiration) and Chekhov, plus a number of modernist stalwarts, along with anecdotes of friends and others, celebrations of the busy works of hands and 'Notebooks', which record his peaceful activism.

In the moving 'Death in Childhood' he writes of a physicist's little boy he met on the beach at La Jolla, who explained a shell to him with great care:

> He had to have been a very avid listener.
> It seemed to me to mean that he'd been loved,
> and wanted to be like his father, which was why
> it was so delicious to him to be talking
> to almost any adult about all there is to know.

It is not surprising, then, that Hass should answer in interview the question 'What is our purpose on earth?' with: 'To express ourselves. To be kind to each other, to meet each other.'

In *Why Poetry Matters* (2008) Jay Parini explored the question of voice, concluding that the High Modernists – Yeats, Frost, Stevens and Eliot – 'all seem to have understood that personality is an invention as much as a discovery'. He quotes Yeats's 'The Mask': 'It was the mask engaged your mind, / And after set your heart to beat, / Not what's behind'. One would put money on Hass's real and poetic selves as being close to identical.

And as for masks…

Liz Byrne

In my other life

In my other life, I draw a line
in the poison, zip my lips, refuse
to swallow a single drop more.

I hang like a bat, sleep upside-down;
eat Magnums for breakfast, toast
with butter and gooseberry jam for dinner.

I sing as if my lungs are my own; dance
on the zebra crossing; play the saxophone
until my lips bleed the blues.

I speak the language of trees, interpret bark,
trace the hieroglyphs of roots. I dye my hair
the shy green of new leaves.

I am deer, hare, fox. I taste the wind with a flare
of nostrils, a flick of ears, a shiver of skin. I lick
my fur smooth, curl in the bracken.

You fall in love with the toast crumbs
in the corners of my mouth, my fluency in oak
and ash, the flash of my white rump.

Gerard Smyth

Pink Moon of April

for P

A pink moon, she says
as she watches through clouds moving together.
A spectacle in the trees, a lucent brilliance
like hanging silk
or a wine glass filled with Chardonnay.

A pink moon drawing close
as if it knows that the earth now needs a mother
like the mother who comes to the child
who wakes up frantic, whose intake
of breath is far too quick after a bad dream.

On the second night she sees it again –
a face in the window looking in.
It is, she says, like the appearance of a friend
not seen for so long.
Not since the world was a different place.

The Hawthorn Way

At the grave of J M Synge

Shall I bring a garland of Wicklow gorse,
stones from Aran, or come with oak leaves
from the oak trees of Glencree.
Shall I recite some lines from *Riders to the Sea*,
sprinkle on your grave water from the wells
of Connemara, or drops of rain collected
from the rain pools of Rathfarnham.

Shall I choose autumn or spring to find your nook,
or at the end of an Indian summer
scatter a handful of backstage dust
along the Hawthorn Way.
How long should I stay, how long should I pause
in contemplation before it's time to go
like Deirdre at the end of *Deirdre of the Sorrows*.

Abegail Morley

Live Stream

"It's not as easy as going back on stage and switching on the lights."
Tamara Rojo, Director, English National Ballet

Outside this life you're playing hide-and-seek
with me, peeling the backbone of shadows
from their stretch. You speak of my puppetry,
strings, hinges, unbraided hair; the tiny drill holes
through fingers and wrists ache in the cold,
and my lonely voice, raising from the slim cord of spine,
taut as childhood violence, pools in the air like a bruise.
And in this cardboard dollhouse and its fake wallpaper
and tiny carved beds, I slam the fake timber door
and it sways like an overcast moon whistling to sky.

In Act II I raise my arms on my own accord,
move across this vacant stage in my spring dress,
poke the front row with a stick. *This is the dress,*
I say as I thrust myself from the wings.
I've lost my audience, but two rows back,
in computer light, you're shuffling on screen
like dripping water and thirty seconds from now,
in this hollow place, my dance will reach
the end of its dark alley and fade, ever so gently
with the stage lights. And you'll stay in your seat
long after lights up just to touch
the horror of me as I exit, strings tangling.

Richie McCaffery

Sugar tongs

Nearly matte black with the grime
of two centuries of handling,
this pair of silver sugar tongs.

The car boot sale's nearly over
so I get them for 50p from a fed-up
seller who thinks they're plated.

In fact they're Georgian silver,
made in Cheapside, London, 1788
by Samuel Godbehere and Edward Wigan.

Engraved with swags and festoons
as well as the family's initials –
polish makes them gleam in no time.

We decide to use them at home
but soon are troubled by their purpose –
to grip nuggets of plantation sugar.

To hold at a distance and not get
your hands dirty while your tea
is sweetened to your liking.

But the silver tarnishes quickly
when it's covered in fingerprints
like those left at the scene of a crime.

House arrest

Her entire street was once housing
for the police force and their family
and now she's a copper's widow,
her husband killed by tobacco
and the murderer still at large.

She's the only remaining link
to why these houses were built
in the first place and her neighbours
just can't see why she's still there,
still under the custody of old love.

Omar Sabbagh

His Final Solution

Dubai in a time of lockdown

Chugging them off
on the dilapidated train
of their pitiless
minds untrained

by any kind of sadness

or not enough
to breed thought
into the bones of
thought as it
thinks its way past
naught past naught

I beget what I can
cosseting a time
of harrows
sent like shards of glass
from a telltale man
whose arching sibilance is
a rival to serpents
at their truest pith
and at
the reaches of
their clueless best.

Behave says the god.
Behave.

The savagery of the blood
chugging down the vein
is not purple though
not blue
but a bird in blue

echoing peace
of a sort that cannot
and that
will not
complain.

The gift now of right
of way at last at
long last I say

thanks to the doubling
spirit for all this grey.
The grey men
have the day.

Amen.

Will Stone

Starlings Bathing

In a bare winter field made up of men
downwind of the Thiepval memorial,
they descend in gangs to blacken
February's furrow pools of pearl and milk.
Hundreds; lifting, dropping, veering,
pestering, preening, plashing, bathing
in feathery electricity and helpless beauty.
Yet it was here the shire boys stepped out,
calves tethered downwind of the whistle,
obeying the cane and unholstered pistol
with the heat of the rum on their throat,
swiftly they slipped into prepared shafts.
Militarized herds were reared to be loved
but they left like the horses, ripped apart,
so oncoming thinkers, researchers, scholars
might sift and sort whatever remains,
handle more gently speeches, assurances,
the scattered porcelain limbs of dolls.
Now the bathers towel down in the breeze,
restored they rise in delirious spirals
directly into the sun, shedding darkness,
cleaned of the blood.

High Tide at Porlock Weir

For Margaret Holroyd

The silent hunter has returned,
the little boats sleep on.
Along the creek her predatory form
uncoils darkly beneath the arch.
She nudges forward the sailboats,
but with anchors stern and aft
they are leashed, unable to advance.
With her swag of momentum,
she overwhelms again the old stones
with their vines of rusting chain,
fleecing the shale, ignoring the cries
of fat crows that hop at her side.
Over marsh grass and the grey bones
of a skiff, her currents consolidate.
She eyes her prey, the shore path,
slips on new land like an evening gown.
But all she stole must be left behind,
as above the oak, a new moon
bright echo of an earlier beauty,
signals her dominion is at an end.
She retreats, but never in disarray,
the paths glisten with awakening,
hulls whisper as she passes.

The Fisherman

Out of dawn,
across the ridge of grey stones
slowly the fisherman comes.
Past the bunker sunk in shale,
the cow guarding its small black sail
and gulls sifting their chances,
eyeing the sea's crevices, what gleams.
Past masts and mud scarred with chains,
dog-sniffed sea-junk, a child's cairn
until the desired place where
only sea and sky remain.
The fisherman places his stool
at the summit of the ridge
as the explorer his nation's flag.
He raises the rod and casts
as day shyly appears beside him.
Facing the infinite, and now perhaps
exempt from pain in his completeness.
Behind him a stiff spring breeze
combs the rain pools left in rowboats
scattered about the quay.

John F Deane

For One who Died of the Coronavirus

See now! the white-lush blossoms of the may
    on the flushed-green hedgerows. But she is gone...
and I would have told her of this world's wonders
    of the eye-bright primrose along the ditch
and the wool-soft catkins on the willow;
    I would have told her of the donkey, standing
in a long stillness. And what of the lights
    and music, of Mozart's rich *Laudate*
Dominum? And then I would have told her
    how her name is written down on heaven's
wedding-breakfast table, how a sunlight beam
    on the tabernacle doors is a blaze of furze
on our commonplace hillside. I would have said:
    'Your being is the purest orchid, buried
but for a season beneath the blanketing
    of briar and fern, of buttercup and thorn...
but you know all that, holding it still
    in the accessible cellars of your mind and heart.'

Dylan Carpenter

Rose Factory

My belly is in the weeds. My knees are in the mud. My hands part the brush.

When I dream, I dream exclusively in surface.

Through a chain link fence, in time, I watch trucks idle in the yard. Their beds empty of order and stock, their engines tsk tsk to nowhere, everywhere.

'Make me,' I whispered once, to a rich comely woman, 'something,' as I peeled her garters down her shins.

There, in her gold room, above the nail-trimmed headboard, a great mirror stretched. In it: A boy, a girl, like tocsin, moaned.

As lifters in white smocks bring trays of thornless roses across the docks, rows of trucks cast headlight beams that do not touch.

What lies inside?

Scissors, masked faces, heaps of leaf and thorn, and the cleaned roses, dyed red, spread out.

Anne Symons

Enclosed

From NHS Advice to the shielded (March 2020)
and *the Ancrene Rule* (13th century)

Your safety and care are our concern

Anchored so the puffing devil
does not pitch you over

You have an underlying disease

The life of a recluse avoids ruin
and escapes injury

Do not leave your home

Choose some elderly woman
to keep the door of your cell

Avoid face to face contact

Listen to the priest, but do not speak
nor sing so he may hear

Do not attend any gathering

Take care when you let blood
do not for the sake of one day lose twelve

Severe symptoms may follow

On Wednesdays and Fridays
content yourself with bread and ale

We've delivered your essentials

Eat no flesh except in great sickness
when you may eat potage without scruple

Avoid religious travel

For the love of God, govern yourself
sit still and say nothing. Wait.

Sue Mackrell

I'm the Girl

I'm the girl that makes the thing
that drills the hole that holds the ring
that drives the rod that turns the knob
that works the thingummybob
        Song made famous by Gracie Fields in the Second World War

My mother made wings for Spitfires
at the aluminium works in Newport,
daring in her slacks and turban.

New friendships lightened the grind
of twelve hour shifts, breaks spent
slicking a Victory roll with a bit of spit,
perfecting a Joan Crawford Bow
with beetroot lipstick,
practising dance steps for
Saturday night at the Miners' Welfare.

Dry patches of skin appeared on her wrists,
(not to worry, all the girls had them)
scaly, itchy, soothed with
Pond's Cold Cream and calamine lotion.

And then her hair
 came out in clumps
    her beautiful auburn
        Veronica Lake waves
blocked the scullery sink,
her scalp red raw and bleeding.

At forty-six
she was dead from cancer.

Was she, too, a war casualty?
Not like the shock of
the Bridgend explosions,
girls her own age gone up in a flash
but killed by slow, malignant, insidious
poison.

James Harpur

Cranborne Woods (17 May, 1994)

for my mother

We stopped the car, ducked below the fence
Felt time unravelling in a revelation
The seconds fall and scatter into thousands

Of tiny saints, a reborn multitude
Flowing past the trees, through pools of sun,
Each earthly form a spirit flame, pure blue.

They watched us drift among them, large as gods,
As if we'd come as part of their parousia
To stay with them forever in these woods.

As time grew darker we slipped away like ghosts
And slowly drove ... towards your death next May
When once again I saw the risen host

Could watch you walking weightlessly among
The welcomers, the gently swaying throng.

(from *Oracle Bones,* Anvil Press, 2001)

Corn Circle

It was the third day after he was dead
His body yet to be consigned to fire
We were marooned in limbo, as becalmed

As the endless days of summer rolling by,
Turning to ash the surface soils of Wiltshire
And shrinking the chalk streams of our valley.

That evening we stood on Pepperbox Hill
Gazing at fields embalmed in golden heat
And there, as if cut from the corn, a circle.

We walked down and picked our way through rows
Towards the solar disc burning in the wheat
And crossed the threshold of the temenos

Entering the benediction of the stasis
The heart of the sun, whirling, motionless.

Gill Learner

Lapwings

The winter cycle-routes of growing up were lined
with ploughland where they massed, backs
the greenish-black of Miss Carter's Oxford gown,
V-sign crests, under-wings flashing clean as a Rinso'd vest.

They mottled the earth, swirled up like half-charred newsprint,
flickered down to tap the ground for worms. We loved
their mating *wit-eeze-wit*, their sky-fall tumbling,
the come-on hum of wings.

Sometimes we propped our bikes by a tasselled hedge,
quartered the field for nesting-scrapes, hoping to tease a hen
into a decoy run, one wing trailed, to lure us from
her freckled eggs or dappled chicks.

We didn't know in early Egypt they were trapped
for children's pets, were carved into Karnak walls
with pinioned wings as symbols of a lower caste; nor that
they flit through myths of Ireland, Wales and ancient Rome.

But, in a dozen years those dwindling cries
might be little but folk memory in English fields.

James Roberts

Rooks

They're playing with the wind again
which throws them backwards
their black fingers splayed
above the feathered and skeletal oaks.
And I'm almost down on my knees
praying that this storm
will not reach too far
into the cracks of our lives.
But this ritual they perform
is the opposite of prayer.
They open themselves
and bare their bony souls
to everything that can be hurled against them,
riding curves impossible to negotiate.
Beneath them floodwater
spreads like a bed sheet,
held down by posts and wires.
Can we nail the world shut
long enough to discover everything,
or, at the first incision,
will the birds burst out
in a ghost-swirl murmuration?
The flock splits in fractal ricochets
each rook a syllable falling from a question.
And I'm wondering if I stand here long enough
will I learn to feel the wind
without wanting to know
what it's saying?

Pen and ink drawing, James Roberts

Patricia McCarthy

James Roberts: *Winged* (NightRiverWood, 2020)

Winged is an exquisite chapbook by established poet and artist, James Roberts, who is 'wired' to 'loneliness' 'being a lover of high places', and whose work is celebrated quite often in *Agenda*. As we are told on the back page: 'These pieces were written and drawn during the lockdown period of the Covid-19 epidemic, when the poet was walking where he lives on the Welsh borders which he knows intimately.' Each poem is 'winged', mirroring the title perfectly both in content, music and in shape.

The lockdown we all now recognise situates these poems both externally and internally, for example 'No traffic on the roads,/ no voices except my own'. 'The birds know that, for the first time,/ in many lives, this place is theirs/... Their talons lock and release'... He asks the telling rhetorical question: 'Can we nail the world shut/ long enough to discover everything?'

This sequence links, and, dare I say, surpasses bird poems most of us know. Think of Keats' nightingale, Shelley's skylark. Only Gerard Manley Hopkins' Windhover', to me, seems on a par with these. Roberts certainly demonstrates Hopkins' idea of the special uniqueness or 'this-ness' or inscape of a thing in his treatment of each bird set in the natural world.

Each of the twelve perfectly-wrought poems focuses on a bird and is accompanied by an equally perfectly-wrought pen-and-ink drawing that captures the movement, magic and mystery of each bird, the multi-textured images hauntingly real, yet like abstract paintings. The focus varies: in the first poem, the 'Kingfisher', 'A little Narcissus fishing/inside yourself for the shadow/ you thought you'd swallowed', the bird is addressed lovingly and intimately as 'you'. It is 'little fire-belly', 'little dripping dagger', 'little water bee' that the poet glimpses only rarely 'while I navigate a river that isn't there'. These are no mere descriptive postcard poems. Elsewhere a bird is viewed in the third person, or occasionally the bird is even given its own voice. The poems can be read on so many subtle metaphoric levels also. The terrible predicament of the homeless swan, personified as a woman 'in her pale evening gown', could be that of a homeless person anywhere, or an immigrant without the necessary language 'Now words are gone'. The poem draws to a close by both poet and swan compassionately and prophetically indicating doom 'listening to eggshells,/ for the helpless who will need us/ when they're born'.

Roberts follows in a very special Welsh tradition; think of George Herbert, poet/priest 1593-1633, foremost of the devotional lyricists, who favoured shaped or pattern poems, which go back to ancient Greek sources and where form is integral to meaning. The latter's well-known poem, 'Easter Wings', with its different line-lengths is shaped into opening and closing wings. More recently, R S Thomas, too, had a passion, like Roberts, for bird-watching which he associated with prayer. Roberts' secular or pagan form of prayer in these poems, each one so intense, so epiphanic, requires slow contemplation. In the last poem which concerns a rook, Roberts admits 'And I'm almost down on my knees/ praying that this storm/ will not reach too far/ into the cracks of our lives' and he continues to show the bird's superiority to humans; it doesn't need prayer: 'this ritual they perform/ is the opposite of prayer'. They courageously 'bare their bony souls/ to everything that can be hurled against them'. Like the existentialists, Roberts implies that they survive without the props of any belief or religion. Similarly delicate reverence and respect is implied for Eastern religions such as Buddhism and Moslems. The kite has 'wings flaring like prayer flags'. 'I'm sure they kissed the ground/ the way all birds do,/ never really coming to earth'. Yet the poet humbly admits he can't do this: 'I think I've forgotten how to touch'. His philosophical acuity is evidenced also in the first poem addressed to the kingfisher:

> We have no choice but to sleep
> When we're awake…

Here are overtones of Colin Wilson, Guridjieff, Ouspensky, and even Eliot himself who – in *Four Quartets* – underlined how not many of us reach full consciousness or awareness in our everyday lives ('for us there is only the trying').

Listen to this, also, in the poem about an owl: 'every living thing is just a song/ in the memory of another'.

Elsewhere the poet seems almost indistinguishable from the birds that he observes and claims so knowingly and poet and bird fold into each other. In the poem 'Heron', 'that Viking longboat of the air', for example, he tries to emulate the heron but falls short, unable to learn 'its rapture-stillness'; he can't keep his footing 'in the way of this spear-fisher/perfectly balanced on rickety stilts'. At one point, even the 'feathered and skeletal' oaks in the storm seem to become birds – the poet's painterly eye always evident in his images, the artist's eye similarly evident in the poems.

In 'Goshawk' his thoughts 'fly from themselves like goshawks' and in the last six lines of the poem the goshawk and poet become one: 'We're shapes imagined by a forest,/ streams flowing through it'. In the owl poem, too, Roberts wants to become the 'white owl', 'ghost translucent against the dark,/ to lean out from a high branch and dive/ into the cracks of the underworld'. In the goshawk poem, even his thoughts change into goshawks: 'All light is dappled, and thoughts/fly from themselves like goshawks'. He and the bird become 'we': 'quiet as air while we fall,/ music echoing from the places/ where we land'.

Startlingly original, memorable images abound: the fog 'clings to the hill like a mourner'; 'floodwater/ spreads like a bedsheet'; the rook has 'black fingers', there are 'funerary curtains of rain'; the golden plover 'row themselves into the sky'.

Back to Roberts belonging very naturally to the Welsh bardic tradition: as David Jones (who hand-wrote the logo and Contents especially for *Agenda* many years ago) attests: 'The bards of an earlier Wales referred to themselves as "carpenters of song"'. And Roberts certainly fits this title, achieving 'the feathered lightness required, / the almost undoing before it's done/ that draws out the shiver/ running through everything'. It is this vital 'shiver' that Roberts achieves so wondrously, obeying the Bardic duty. He breathes in the *awen* (the old Welsh word for 'poetic art') and catches his poems in 'the outbreath'. Ironically, this does not stop him asking if he will ever get beyond the need for language, imbibing only its music maybe, at the very end of the sequence:

> And I'm wondering if I stand here long enough
> will I learn to feel the wind
> without wanting to know
> what it's saying?

John Greening

Robert Selby, *The Coming-Down Time* (Shoestring Press, 2020)

It's no surprise to find Shoestring publishing Robert Selby's debut collection *The Coming-Down Time*, since John Lucas, who runs the press, is highly attuned to questions of Englishness, having written an excellent book on the subject. Yet it's perhaps not quite the thing these days for a British poet to explore such questions, or to be preoccupied with a particular corner of England. Yes, Alice Oswald's Devon poems are rightly admired, Penelope Shuttle continues to conjure Cornish spirits, but we no longer reach with confidence for those (largely male) celebrants of English locality whose names once dominated the anthologies. The danger has always been that such poets are not regarded 'like some valley cheese, /local, but prized elsewhere'; rather, they are dismissed as parochial – as were Norman Nicholson, Charles Causley and even the admirable Patricia Beer. The best have come close to satisfying Auden's criteria – Charles Tomlinson (the Potteries and Gloucestershire), Peter Redgrove (Cornwall), C. H. Sisson (Somerset), Geoffrey Hill (West Midlands), Simon Armitage (Yorkshire) – but the greatest will rise out of their own locality, going way beyond it, yet taking their readers along. Think of a certain Nobel Prize-winning Irish poet – still known and loved in his home long after he stopped digging childhood bogs, when he had passed Station Island, out to *Beowulf* and Book VI of *Aeneid*.

Selby's poetry has no obvious resemblance to any of the above-mentioned English writers, only a couple of whom are much loved or even known in their own 'patch'; and while he draws on the Georgians, he doesn't fall back on their now archaic tropes. Nevertheless, those 'Forefathers' of Edmund Blunden's (and Blunden was a Kentishman like Selby) are in the distant shadows from the outset:

> He came from a long line of men who worked
> now-extinct equine trades: wheelwright, ostler,
> coachman, horseman. His groom father begat
> nine in the 'coming-down time'.

Heaney is also there, but refreshingly Selby avoids sounding anything like him, and has learnt more from MacNeice about how to maintain a brisk, no-nonsense tone without losing the burnish (it's not often mentioned how brilliantly MacNeice wrote about the English landscape, quite avoiding the shades of Romantic forebears). Another expatriate Irish poet, Bernard

O'Donoghue, is to be found praising these poems on the back of Shoestring's elegantly designed volume, and he's quite right to call it 'a marvellous anatomy of English life'. He might even have quoted Kavanagh's 'Epic', the battle-cry for all local-universal poets.

The first of *The Coming-Down Time*'s three sections is the twenty-part 'East of Ipswich', a Suffolk sequence which plunges us straight into family history, but never abandons us to personal nostalgia or impenetrable private myth. How reassuring to realise that a poem is not titled 'Oxford', as first appears, but 'Orford'. The presiding spirit here is more Crabbe than Arnold, more Crossley-Holland than Motion. These are real, experienced landscapes with living figures in them, and there's none of the ethereal philosophising that, say, American poets tend to summon in the wilderness. Even the wildest English vista, after all, is likely to have signs of life – an old firing range, a tumulus, a dry-stone wall, a forgotten battlefield, some ridge-and-furrow, a church spire, a wind turbine, and a high-end hotel. Selby knows this, and doesn't pretend that things are otherwise; mercifully, he knows how to place such features within his landscapes and to make music with them, continually shaping his verses so that they have all the virtues of good prose. He allows room for local 'phrase and fable', anecdotes, off-the-cuff remarks, but is always observing:

> Behind him as he pedals on,
> his white twill shirt too sweat-stuck to billow,
> the gods turn and face the final furrow.

There are many such quotably felicitous phrases ('a smaller world/ stitched by jets'), touches of humour and humanity, but Selby never loses track of his structures, or abandons his forms, taut and tensile. History keeps pushing at the verse: the grandfather's WW2 experience, especially. If the individual stories don't quite rise to a broader significance, that is not to undervalue the impression they make. Their very simplicity – though it shares a party wall with banality ('My grandmother,/making jelly for the trifle...' 'the record player/that, later, became a CD player') – can be moving, as in the five-line 'sestet' of the unconventional sonnet, 'When That Which is Perfect is Come':

> Her maiden name, the name
> of the most famous Kentish beer hop,
> was gone; so too, eventually, were the hops,
> the green rows blackening with *Verticulum*
> *Wilt*, one-by-one, until the kells cooled.

That last cadence is superb, combining the chill Latin pest name with discreet pauses ('one-by-one') before the brilliantly specific chime of 'kells cooled'.

Although 'East of Ipswich' makes a heart-warming and readable opening to the collection, the book's middle section, 'Shadows on the Barley' is more wide-ranging, consisting chiefly of individual poems. Selby seldom strays for very long from the Kentish Weald, winter woods, elms, cherries, jays, cattle, church spires, but there are visits elsewhere, to Scotland, London, even Maine. Several poems are retrospective and maintain the elegiac mood of the first section, notably 'Upon the Altar Laid', a longish piece which remembers veterans of WW1. In fact, I was reminded once again of Blunden in 'The Sycamore', which describes how a smithy's boy propped his bike against the tree and headed for the trenches, leaving it to grow on while history advances through Passchendaele:

Long since the blacksmith sold off the yard,
since war ended, resprouted, withered again,
and the Trossachs became a National Park,
the bicycle protrudes still, a man-made limb
mimicking new growth. The ribbed handlebars
wait for young hands to re-clasp them,
pull free of the frame and tour off, roadworthy,
this cast-iron memorial in the skyward lee.

Four poems on 'The Galilean Moons' might seem to offer an ambitious broadening of scope, but these are moons as seen from mission control in Kent or Suffolk. Selby is happiest communing with the elders of the Weald ('Dear Ralph Crozier'), or imagining how a Victorian entomologist might watch his wife, or telling 'The Land Girl's Story', or joining Hardy 'Outside Elizabeth Endorfield's'. But this section of the book has poems which seem to move in the bolder direction he develops in Section 3, emphasising the rawly personal and the contemporary, if not quite as surprisingly as they might. A poem titled 'Lady Thatcher' proves to be about a lady thatcher ('At elevenses, she comes down/for a builder's tea and a sandwich'), although there is a subtle political undercurrent in the book as a whole.

The location of the final sequence, as it happens, was much in the news when *The Coming-Down Time* was published during the early weeks of the global pandemic. The Prime Minister had retired to his official Kentish manor and was much criticized in the press. Selby's 'Chevening' takes epigraphs from Ivor Gurney and Eliot ('History is now and England' – what else?) to tell a modest love story in twelve parts, acted out amid 'a rich man's flowering lawns' against a history of colonial wars and a fraught Englishness, where life 'is at the pace a picnic blanket unfurls'. These are country-house poems, part of a long tradition, although the poet here is very much the day-tripping everyman ('our weekend in my country') taken up with his own quotidian concerns. Yet so was Ben Jonson when he visited Sidney's Penshurst. I think both Jonson and the author of 'Astrophil and Stella' would have recognised what Selby is doing:

> In the arboretum, under palms gifted
> by diplomats at dim-distant summits
> grown gaunt now with uncongenial climes,
>
> you looked each way twice
>
> then pressed me against the hot, red brick.
> Your hair was slow through my fingers,
> tasting salty, smelling of Ambre Solaire.

As a sequence of love poems, this works very well, formally varied, and enriched by a pervasive quasi-elegiac mood – not quite nostalgia, but a powerful sense of what has gone before. As the epigraph suggests, Eliot provides the model, and the opening ('Will you enter/the maze with me?/ Do you trust me to find the/way/to the centre of things') could be an offcut from one of the *Four Quartets*. But Selby has a better eye than Eliot for the details of English rural life, 'the cake stalls and book stalls', and an instinctive gift for pastoral – the way, for instance, the visitor from London returns from Kent 'treading Downs dust/and pollen into its pavements'.

Will Stone

Richie McCaffery: *First Hare* (Mariscat Press, 2020)

In the poem 'Balancing the books' from his collection *Passport* (Nine Arches Press, 2018) Richie McCaffery laments with a modicum of rue 'I spend too much of my time in old bookshops' and in another 'Day in the Life', he continues 'I spend my days in the library researching dead poets'. One might imagine McCaffery is opining that he ought to be somewhere else when in fact he is doing what true poets have always done, like Rilke ensconced in the Bibliothèque Royale in Paris, i.e. sought out their kinsmen. For the bookshop and library are McCaffery's natural and rightful domain. Here he secures rare volumes and studies how poets, if not the unacknowledged legislators of the world, can at least claim to be the sharp-eyed articulators of life, scalpel poised over their generation or epoch. And like them McCaffery is one of the few poets I observe today who manages to spotlight existence in a narrow beam as it passes between the darkness of past and future.

In the curiously named poem from *Passport* 'Baudelopark', which sounds like the author of 'Une Charogne' were severed mid appellation, the poet states 'The days pass by and barely make eye contact with me.' That may be, but what is more important is that this ever lucid, witty, razor-wire sharp, deceptively playful and achingly truthful poet most certainly attempts to make eye contact with them, subjecting them to an interrogative gaze, never letting them off the hook. McCaffery is that rare poet who turns over stones others nonchalantly pass by, a seer of the everyday, of life lived, who manages to exalt the bric-a-brac of living to a poignant message of both a resilience against and acceptance of the absurdities universally common to existence. His bitter-sweet evocations of loss expose what lies beneath those stones, and since his debut proper *Cairn* (Nine Arches Press, 2014) McCaffery has I would argue carved out a niche in which there is only room for his peculiar insight and beautifully crafted verses, which seem as smooth and finished as if worked on a lathe, prohibiting over production, no frills. As here in the poem 'Step Father' from *Cairn*.

> A place of abandoned colliery terraces,
> their roofs slowly caving in to beams
> holding dirty huddling pigeons,
> their petrol slick plumage
> mimicking the shades of lost slates.

McCaffery's latest offering is *First Hare*, a richly crafted chapbook from Mariscat Press. The cream cover shows the dark imprint of a hare's profile in mid-leap, presumably to the afterlife since the creature is accompanied by lush crimson blood smudges. Aesthetically I am taken back to McCaffery's beautifully illustrated *Ballast Flint* from 2013, published through the Cromarty Arts Trust after his period as poet in residence. Where *Passport* deals with the challenges of life lived as a spiritual enjambement between his native Northumberland and Flanders, *First Hare* is evidently more anchored in the home country, a return to roots after the ongoing dislocation of living latterly in Ghent. We have at the close of the poem 'The atheists' a glimpse of the new domain, but is this merely a place to 'stay', not to 'live'? Is the spectre of discomposure not to be expunged?

> We live in an old part of town, by evening only
> the main road's lit and the street where we stay
> and the countryside beyond is swaddled in dark
> as if all human faith and knowledge
> is this narrow way, losing grip by the hedgerows.

Yet the shadows of his adopted country still pass over the text like cloud shadows fleeting over a field of ripening English corn, most tellingly perhaps in the fine poem 'La Merle Blanc' which concerns one of McCaffery's long-held passions, antique fountain pens. Ostensibly about the curious renaming of a pen made in England later exported to Belgium, the poem cleverly serves as an analogy for McCaffery's recent past of disconnection and like so many of his other poems, subtly explores the values of rootedness and rootlessness, testing the glass ceiling of continental migratory reality within the protective fetters of the familial bloodline. The poem ends with a sigh of hope, albeit for the pen's future, not our own, through the satisfying image of the pen's healthily flexing gold nib as bird beak.

> We are the produce of one nation
> packaged for another, and unlike
> the politics of our times
>
> this pen's gold beak of a nib
> has such a beautiful flex to it.

In another poem 'Falling' we are also back in Belgium, at Flanders fields and World War I, yet through the prism of one of the poet's family members, strangely prone to falls. This comical device acts as an unassuming lighter vertebrae on which to hang something weightier. McCaffery's great grandfather was a sniper at Ypres but survived through his good fortune in literally falling out of the way of danger. Having been shot in the shoulder and fallen out of a tree before even firing his snipers' rifle, he caught a Blighty one but ...

> Later in a riveter's brace on the Tyne
> he plummeted into the bowels of a liner.

> He worked so hard to bring his family up a peg;
> this made his drunken dive more spectacular.

The poem by including the word Tyne, suggests the vast Commonwealth military cemetery near Zonnebeke known as Tyne Cot after the soldiers of the Northumberland regiment who lent this name to their impossible objective, the smoking ruins of the 'cots' on the German held ridge of Passchendaele.

Yet *First Hare* announces the homecoming from the off with 'Northumbrian', and its telling line 'We move so much I sometimes think we must be stolen goods.' The poem deals with the poet and his Flemish wife's urgent desire for stability in the new rural surroundings of his motherland, the image of two people wishing to be locked naturally together like the stones in the dry-stone wall they are admiring without need of mortar or cement, is poignant. Then the hare is sighted. The poem ends on what may be inferred as an ominous note, the sense of something inwardly precious being unknowingly prepared for an assault by external reality.

> Our love fattens itself daily
> unaware of greater schemes at play.

Another revealing poem is 'The Fork', which sees the poet engrossed in a dull domestic task, on hands and knees in the plot of his 'cul de sac home', clearing the gutter of leaves when an invitation comes to attend a high school reunion. The juxtaposition of the predicament of whether to attend or not with the eccentric drain-clearing implement, a Georgian cutlery fork with deer antler handle, creates an unlikely tension and unforeseen poetic dividend. McCaffery's gift is to serve something which appears light but harbours something richer and heavier. By taking a simple prop, a story, a memory, an anecdote, the poet then conducts this narrow tributary into the wider estuary of revelation. Yes, he does this with a language which is notably spare but such lean verse is also cleverly strewn with hidden traps beneath the camouflage of conversation, as here in 'The atheists':

Boredom brings me to St Peter's, an exhibition
of nativity scenes from around the world,
variations on a set theme all with the same sign:
Do not touch, which is apt – I don't want to
and they don't touch me as well.

This nothing wasted, Jack Sprat approach exacerbates the effect of the revelatory-impulse; the reader is irresistibly drawn into the poem by the intriguing, the charming or familiar, like an unsuspecting insect unknowingly heading towards the centre of a web. But at some point something dark pounces, bundling the visitor into a sticky silk and holding them there while the killer image is played before them, as that in 'Dead man's beer', with those 'thirty yellow-black tins of Boddingtons, like a nest of wasps, their presence stinging his widow.'

As already indicated old books and their capacity for summoning ghosts or dispensing long-held secrets prove the ideal material for McCaffery's musings on existence and in the poem 'Certificates' he stumbles on the official evidence of his own birth 'quite by accident, stuffed into a half-read book, about to be sent to the charity shop.' The irony here is that the old book, whose fate is to be moved on to the charity shop, paradoxically bears the huge responsibility of containing the proof of existence of a human being. The condemned book carries the birth certificate inside it somewhere else, away from the one whose existence it proves. The second part of the poem concerns a found death certificate, a clever counterpoint and the blackly comic prospect of McCaffery having to deal with a fractious ghost searching for proof of his own extinction prevents him from binning it, just in case. This poem perfectly illustrates the delicious rhythm of contrasts, the push and pull affect, the dark and the light, warmth and coldness, the forgotten and the recalled, presence and oblivion, which are the veins and capillaries that serve McCaffery's vision. Returning to *Passport* and 'Balancing the Books', the reader can observe how these channels converge to supply and maintain the pulse of a poet who should be far better appreciated in this country for his precious alchemy, the interweaving of simplicity and complexity. Now is surely the time to savour this eloquent interlocuter of our shared existence.

I take a book off the shelf
and splay its pages
like a pigeon-fancier with
a prize bird, knowing fine well
it might never make it home.

Elizabeth Ridout

Kate Miller, *The Long Beds* (Carcanet Press, 2020)
Belinda Cooke, *Stem* (The High Window, 2020)
Katrina Naomi, *Wild Persistence* (Seren, 2020)
Maria Taylor, *Dressing for the Afterlife* (Nine Arches Press, 2020)
Pascale Petit, *Tiger Girl* (Bloodaxe Books, 2020)

The new reality in which we find ourselves places the homestead as a site of not comfort, warmth or control, but of imprisonment. The fascinating and terrible world of lockdowns and enforced domestication is hardly a new one to women – existing in a place of permanent escape from or prey to its poisonous attractions. In a state of incarceration, one can turn inwards and explore the eternal internal, or one can apply a new lens and examine the minutiae of the everyday, to find the poetic in the prosaic. The best poet links both to win their freedom.

Kate Miller's *The Long Beds* takes apart the homely or domestic space, and renders it a point of adventure, a place fit for "great reckonings in a little room". The bed, that representative of so much, is transformed into a site of travel or passage. In this, the most repressive and obviously marital or domestic of objects, the poet is free to travel worlds. Her pieces have the quality of lucid dreaming – take place between the state between asleep and awake – a liminal space which works so well in the present time. Miller uses language in an almost Pre-Raphaelite way – the exquisite detail of the small and delicate things which make up the whole form poems which work as a patchwork quilt of lives, times, and references. Linen and bedding are often referred to: "sheets and towels must wait for their ablution…redeemed in the perpetual lifting and laying-on of hands" – a source of female drudgery. Miller takes the site of the mundane or domestically dirty and makes it exciting. She uses the humanising vulnerability of sleep to explore the writing of new lives and times, merging self-exploration from a single site with a poetic capacity to travel eras and continents internally. Sheets, of course, are also paper, as explored in 'Woman of Letters' and 'Turned Down':

> The lid is off a heavy jar of spider leggy ink.
> I wait to see her free those spiders when she writes
> her wiry black left-handed script. They run
> amok across the sheets.

To this great effect, Miller uses the language of ships and the sea. The bed, the pivotal point of the collection, floats upon a sea of dreams. Miller's conceit of a bedstead surviving a bombing to protect what is underneath it in an almost motherly way works well here – the bed becomes a ship with cargo underneath on which the reader and poet travel through and across time beginning with her masque piece:

> In a robe of *thunder*-colour; her crazy hair, a Circle of Crows before Cloud;
> in her hand a paper cup, with two *Pills*, a *white*, a *red*.

These dreamlike stagings of the mind merge to celebrate the nursing night staff at King's College hospital. The bed transports us to a series of islands, each a site of Tempest-like dreams. The narrative of Miranda, now Queen of Naples, is a fitting one – linking dreams to bees which in turn links us to the matriarch, the queens of dreams Miller is visiting one by one:

> The time I had to shoo him off, Cal only wanted me,
> with my small hands, to steal honeycomb.
> So close we came to blows, the bees were roused,
> a thousand eyes and *twangling instruments*.

The Muriel sequence uses these objects to tell stories which weave in and out of dreams, such as 'Speaking Voice' and 'School Prize 1912'. The pieces move from the Raj, overwhelmingly colourful and intense but transitory and evasive, to the Waterloo Bridge series, in which the silence of sleep is broken by morning or awakening. The bridge as a liminal space between dream and reality works as a site from which to explore London; that transformative, bombed, rebuilt organism, exploring the bridge's experiences from Dickens to the prostitutes of the Thames to the struggles of World War II. As we begin the day, we begin to make our mark and move out of silence and sleep – as seen in 'Song of Sunrise':

> oh ladies, ladies. Morning light, leaves, flowers on the banks,
> The promises you meant for us.

The Thames has always been considered a place of sea changes and transformation and is no different in Miller's last poems – like the morning, when we can rewrite our yesterday and begin to make our mark afresh, even in the darkest of times.

Belinda Cooke's *Stem* is full of good, life-affirming, earthy poems. The everyday is explored with the true poet's lust for life – 'early waking', 'Sunday morning', 'connections that are more complicated than we think'. Cooke has truly changed her lens to the zoom – seeing the world in high definition, close up and appreciative. These poems are tiny points, apertures of appreciation. Cooke is 'glad to embrace the day/ on this if not the best of days':

> I'd like to draw a life for you – a room of endless music,
> heart's ease, surf distant, incoming tide
> neither owned or disowned
> as we hold down the focus button.

Cooke is 'sharp as a snowdrop/with a macrolens'. The beauty to be found in the normal, the seemingly trivial which can, in the light of tragedy, be realised as so important – is seen everywhere – a 'Paul McCartney song', 'sitting in Annie Aldridge's kitchen' – these are strong, rootsy poems:

> Just when we've nearly got used to
> things being pointless, a moment comes
> in and slaps us in the face

Cooke's convent girl pieces address memory – they have a sharpness to them which offsets the appreciative like lemon juice in a cake – 'rebirth, rising…desperate coffee.' Cooke recognises that the connections of routine or the familiar are how we time travel. The mental and the practical in these pieces sometimes jar and are more often beautiful:

> while the Council Tax lady wants to know
> where exactly is our matrimonial home –
> but morning brings Rilke barefoot
> in dew-covered grass, with static white noise

– concluding with the simultaneously funny and terrible musing – 'what will I do if life is just okay?' There are many pieces on walking or walks, including the lovely 'Shiplake Walk with Alan':

> you both no longer scientists till you
> spot Red Kites along river toll paths and sides of crops
> then amicably back through Sonning church
> edging towards our leisurely state.

Cooke's psychogeographic appreciation reflects upon the beauty of both the pointless and the practical – closing with 'Woodburning Stove' reminds us of the need to appreciate, to see afresh – especially when these things can, so suddenly, be taken from us:

> Daily you saw the wood
> and load it in the stove.
> Evenings I come home
> lie back, take in the heat.

In a similar vein, Katrina Naomi's *Wild Persistence* explores the creative and emotional life of a wonderfully ordinary woman. These poems are deeply touching and often very funny – 'How to Celebrate a Birthday', 'On Fucking':

> We have gone for days –
> a week, or two has been known –
> and the inevitability is palpable,
> why haven't we done this to ourselves?

This collection is her first since moving to Cornwall and it shows – the pace is different. A change of focus allows the sense of freedom and space to make new artistic and life decisions. Cornwall herself features heavily in these poems – :

> Saints are all about her. Herring and mackerel
> flit from the frothing nets of underskirts… as the tidal collars retreat,
> choughs fix their nests
> in her windy hair, their bright legs and beaks
> ornament. This is a dress for accordions and fiddles.
> This is a dress for a storm.

She fits well into Naomi's manifesto of inclusivity – Cornwall is wild, not just picturesque. In 'Dualism: a Manifesto', Naomi launches a conscious tirade to live all parts of one's life and embrace all parts of the self and of life:

> Think what I could achieve by
> splitting myself
> one hand
> one side of the brain to write or paint
> the other to perform

the mundane jobs
that persist in
winking at me
God got greedy
choosing to be three people
Let's have no truck with that
At once I could be
the one who vogues to Eurovision
in orange sequinned stilettoes
and the other who reads
yet another Iris Murdoch
in cream and brown brogues.

Wild Persistence contains much fabulous detail and a number of very powerful pieces. The series of poems dealing with rape narrative is extremely powerful, but, tellingly, does not define the narrative, which is *her* narrative, not her rapist's. Naomi's new space in Cornwall is leading her to new artistic forensics – shown prettily in 'Elemental', stealing mud from the boots of men to possess herself fully in this new land. Despite this prettiness, the collection bristles with inspiring, complex female figures – for instance, 'Boasting Sonnet', and 'Mentor'. The women of this collection are spared from the trappings of domesticity which breeds definition so well:

I told the man I wasn't impressed
when he unwrapped an ordinary duster –
you know, the fluffy yellow kind –
and there was a dark, almost Bakelite shape
something toy about it, and squat –
a toad is more attractive

Naomi does not only embrace, she rejects – university, London, organised religion, children. Her poems are anarchic and colourful – like Cornwall.

In contrast to this colour and freewheeling, Maria Taylor's *Dressing for the Afterlife* is elegant. These poems, a series of reflections on how memory and object transports us through time, have a cinematic, Hollywood-soft-focus feel. Taylor begins with an exploration of running through and from past existences and definitions of herself to a hope of freedom – but it remains a hope. 'She Ran':

I ran through the screaming wind, rain and cloud.
I ran through my mother's village and flew past
armed soldiers at the Checkpoint. I ran past
my grandparents and Bappou's mangy goats
with their mad eyes and scaled yellow teeth.

Dressing for the Afterlife acts as a box of images and visitors to the mind. It is full of iconography – religious and cinematic, past selves, the moon, Ophelia. Taylor is fascinated by the binaries and parallels of the self, as illustrated by 'Moon in Gemini':

tonight our eyes won't meet
tonight they will
tonight you'll think of the past
drown in neon
tonight a woman in a mirror says, 'go home'
don't listen

Taylor uses iconography and representatives to explore the possibilities of moving away from the archetypes we construct around ourselves, as in 'Role Model':

Neither Thelma or Louise, nor side-saddled
on a milk-white horse through Death Valley
nor a fashionista, a sweet-tooth for luxury
statement heels, a homicidal stiletto thing
nor Julie Andrews with a guitar, the whiskers
the kittens, the woman who's holy water

Taylor shows a liberating dissolution of these 'images of floating items' but is ultimately beautifully dubious as to whether this is sustainable – 'your name rises from the water'. Water is, as we have seen, a site of transmogrification – for Taylor, it is in the Heraclitean sense. These transformations continue into pieces such as 'Poem In Which I Lick Motherhood' – the transformations, noise and iconography of motherhood dissolves into a puddle of words:

I am constructed from sticky-back tape, pipe cleaners and clothes
pegs.There are instructions for making me. Look at the appropriate
shelves in reputable stores. I am fascinated by bunk beds, headlice and
cupcakes. You will only leave the table when I have given you clear
instructions.

Taylor's pieces are often funny – 'Hypothetical', 'Friday at the Moon', 'How To Survive a Disaster and More'. The pieces prickle with recognition:

If you must have sex be quick
Be attentive to the fluctuations of accidental music.
Lick your thumb and read the weather.
Ensure you're with the right survivors.
On the face of it hold nothing dear.

Taylor uses multiple references to maps – a clever conceit allowing you to choose your own poem, choose your own ending. These choices or tensions between a desire to shed oneself and the inability to do so often plunge the collection into the difficult ordinary – such as 'Not About Hollywood' and 'Unfinished Business'. Ultimately, 'the moon's a romantic image/often swallowed whole', and 'one day I will be old/ and one day you will be old – but we won't be the same'. Taylor ends this strong collection with 'Woman Running Alone', and a joyful lack of closure on whether old selves can ever truly be escaped.

Pascale Petit always brings us feminist ecopoetics unlike anyone else. In *Tiger Girl*, the endangered woman of the title acts as a site of interaction, sometimes troubled, sometimes joyful, always beautiful. Britain meets India in her newest and strongest collection yet, a postcolonial exploration of the ransacking of both heritage and the natural world. 'Barn owls' meet 'rupees' meet 'flames' meet 'lampblack' – the Tiger Girl is at once Petit, her grandmother and the women of India – but also a site to explore the ethics of environmental and cultural extinction, being predator and prey all at once:

The tigress has passed by now, and is ahead on the path,
rolling over the sand, belly-up, revelling in her power.
Already she's spawned three sets of cubs
and they've forged their own empires...
When I've firewalked through the dawn of your death
my feet scorched
on the cinder path to your house,
when I've opened the gate to your garden –
like opening the gate to Tala Zone
where wildlife is almost safe –
I will land in your armchair in the deepest cave.

The enticing and challenging landscape of India mirrors the personalities of the strong and yet vulnerable woman – spanning from Kew Gardens to Central India:

> I love the boiler and wooden tongs, the mangle
> rollers that I turn and turn, to go back
> to my Gran's as she takes in neighbours washing
> until everything shines like the giant wood spider webs
> I found in Bandhavgarh jungle
> strung between sal and dhok trees swaying in the sun like sheets hung to dry,
> and her at the centre – the Monday morning of my life.
> Petit's creation of "Tiger Gran", a perfect mix of the vulnerable and 'exotic':
> My tawny grandma with as many wrinkles as tributaries
> in the Ganges, her face the map of India when its summer,
> the map of Wales in winter. And sometimes her wrinkles
> are stripes that scare me if I look at her
> when she is flying the tails of her stories.
> She who was left to run wild by her doting father
> when she wasn't slaving for his white family.

Her grandmother represents a ferocious protection from Petit's exploration of sexual exploitation and vulnerability at the hands of the predatory males who stalk this collection; her father's and her great-grandfather's – 'After my father came in while I was sleeping / and lay on top of me as if I was nothing / but a riverbed he needed to flow over – / I dreamt of fishes with children's faces.' The women discussed here are both outside and inside the tiger and what it represents. Strong yet vulnerable animals prowl the pages- the tiger, the fruitbat, the peacock.

The 'Tiger Gran' pieces sing of an extinction of a type of woman, and a type of existence – the damage of globalisation and mass consumption damaging the world, and the Tiger Girl; both Petit and her grandmother, straddlers of oceans:

> Only when I drove through rural India
> did I see the women, all rod-backed,
> balancing firewood on their heads,
> a hay-bale, four bags of cement –
> only then did I see her carrying me, not
> in her womb, but on her head, held high
> over the Channel as she walked
> through water to take me to safety.
> Some of the strongest pieces in the collection are direct in their addressing

of ecological as well as emotional decay and damage – 'ExtinctionRebellion' and 'Flash Fires':

> The day will come when papers
> will only tell leaf stories
> of blackbirds' quarrels with sparrows.
> Their pages will roll back into trees
> and the front page will be bark.
> Tabloids will be hundred-winged birds
> singing earth anthems.

'Pangolin' (Orignally published in the recent 'Pound Reconsidered' issue of *Agenda*), in the wake of the current Covid-19 pandemic, proves terrifyingly Ovidian as danger is shown to change and mutates both within us and within the natural world, a warning we can and should all take in the current landscape we find ourselves in:

> one pangolin, perhaps the last.
> Tell me, you who do not believe in Aryans
> who once pronounced themselves
> the master race, and thought others to be subhuman,
> what is the mastery that makes us
> drive other races, other species, to extinction?

Genevieve Stevens

Laura Scott: *So Many Rooms* (Carcanet, 2019)

Laura Scott does not rush or fuss as she shows us around her many rooms. Her voice is poised and patient, containing within its quiet dignity the burden of experience. We follow Scott through this collection with the reassuring sense that these poems have known themselves a long time; their finely tuned music, their formal conviction – largely measured out in regular couplets, tercets and quatrains – and their astonishing attention to detail come from the mind of someone who has spent a lot of time looking at her world in both sorrow and rapture. Perhaps that is why *So Many Rooms*, Scott's first full-length book, is so compelling – its perceptual signature feels hard-won and authentic. There are no short cuts here, no sentiment overblown or grand flourishes of discovery. Words come under a door 'like rats squeezing themselves / flat', a child sits in a tree 'while the branch moves up and down / like a horse under your weight', while another child watches unseen as grown ups 'swirled and whirled and married the wrong people'. Even when Scott pushes language dangerously close to cliché, for example the use of 'heavy heart' in 'A Different Tune', she reinvigorates the metaphor by addressing her literal heart:

> Shall I make a sling for you of silk and fingers
>
> in a blue that brings out your bruised red?
> I could hang it from the bony strut
>
> of my collarbones to hammock your sad weight.

The opening poem, 'If I could write like Tolstoy' positions itself on the unsteady ground of the conditional, in the mind of someone both longing for greater possibility and acutely aware of her own short falls. This is familiar territory for Scott's narrator; throughout the collection she is tormented by a certain sense of her own inadequacy: 'my lack, my heaving lack, the one I carry on my back / that's what I know that's what I write' she laments in 'What I Know'. This perpetual recourse to something missing, something wanting brought to mind Ruskin's description of artists as those who 'feel themselves wrong': 'The more beautiful the art', he writes, 'the more it is essentially the work of people who feel themselves wrong – who are striving for the fulfilment of the law, and the grasp of loveliness, which they have not yet attained.' Scott is unarguably a poet who 'feels herself wrong'.

Yet armed with such deft skill she is able to use this profound sense of lack to unsettle her poems, to energise them with possibility. Where better to explore questions of identity, place, beauty and loss than from the fault line of lack and fulfilment, knowing and doubt, words and silence?

'Breaking Things' beautifully demonstrates this sense of inadequacy. In it, the narrator recalls how she dropped a variety of significant objects during her childhood: precious china, milk bottles, her grandmother's bowls 'soft and grey – all my mother had left. She cried / when I broke one and even then, I understood why.' This event, marked with failure and regret, fuels the narrator's longing to hold onto things, to protect the shape of the past by listening to, and responding to the singularity of her own voice:

> I want to be
> in that inlet where
>
> if I stop listening to you , for a moment,
> I can feel the wake
>
> of a boat slapping against
> the helm of my mind.
>> ('Cove')

Embedded beneath this desire for greater self-understanding is a terrible sadness and rage. Next to one poem in particular, titled 'Can't Stand Them', I've written (and underlined) in the margin VERY GOOD AT HATE. The poem describes the narrator's loathing of hydrangeas, 'with their heads as big as cabbages / obsequiously bowing to me... I like it when the rain bruises their tiny petals.' This amplified voice, curt and cutting, is so compelling that I found myself wanting to hear it more; Scott on the attack, her language unashamedly spiky, is a wonderfully noisy counterbalance to the collection's lyrical discretion.

And there's the sadness, a chronic soreness grooved into the timbre of this collection. For Scott, tribulation is the fear and/or reality of lost girls, murdered girls, raped girls, girls being dragged from ponds – and it's the grief of the mother who looks on, who must somehow live on:

> And a mother
> a poor mother
>
> out in the night
> dragging her daughter

pulling her out of the water
holding her up
waiting, waiting
for the breath to come. (Falling)

In 'Photograph of Two Girls', the narrator describes the unbearable scene of two young girls hanging: 'They hung them high up. Girl cousins split between / the branches of a great mango tree'. Men cut them down ' – some of them the same men who / found the girls the night before in the fields, who helped them / down and split them open, who shared them out as if they were / fruit to be scraped out of their skins.' Scott writes *into* this suffering, whether it is hers or tragedy she bears witness to, as a way of memorialising lost, drowned, battered lives and as a way of asserting presence and words where there is silence. In one of the most moving poems in the collection, 'Daughter', the narrator reflects on the role of writing when faced with the utter hopelessness of grief:

I am like damp sand collapsing into itself
trying to remember the heel of a girl

now swimming in the sea. All I can do
is make lines for her to shimmer in.

For Scott, certainty, fulfilment, conviction dwell in the past, a time in history 'where the myths are still / soft when they leave your lips', a time when all these lost lives were thriving still. It gives the collection a heavy backwards look – raised only momentarily by poems such as 'Buster Keaton', light in their thinking and turn of phrase:

Look at him
adjusting his hat, finding the balance.

Blameless eyes looking straight at you
as the house collapses around him,
blessing him with his open window.

So Many Rooms is a rich and beguiling book of poems, precisely crafted and delicately held. Scott has seen, deciphered, orchestrated and practiced her dance of restraint and release down to the most subtle of steps. It's also a collection that leaves you wanting – the book equivalent to that shy, thoughtful person at a party you wish you'd spent more time with.

Intelligent eyes.

Personally, I hope that this is the first of many Laura Scott collections, and I look forward to seeing if her tight hold on form and volume might, over time, loosen enough to allow in a few rogue moves and more playful dynamics. For now though, there is a lot to admire in *So Many Rooms,* a brave and profoundly human testament to a life dedicated to the act of looking at what is there, what is just out of reach and what is lost.

W S Milne

Wake Up Call

John Kinsella, *Brimstone: a book of villanelles* (Arc Publications, 2020)
Sean O'Brien, *It Says Here* (Picador Poetry, 2020)
Patricia McCarthy, *Whose hand would you like to hold* (Agenda Editions, 2020)

Australian poet John Kinsella's *Brimstone* could be called a Green poem. It comprises sixty-eight villanelles, and the form he has chosen suits his subject of ecological destruction and extinction of species in an ironic fashion: 'seasons undoing seasons', 'the damaged river', 'chemical warfare', 'green algal bloom' poisoning the water with its toxins, 'the encounters with humans' of shy natural species leading to global health problems in the current pandemic.

A villanelle is a rustic song or dance (from the Latin and Italian) with repeated refrains. Kinsella sticks rigidly to the nineteen line structure of the form, although he breaks tradition a little (the English tradition, that is) by breaking the lines up into stanzas (although Dylan Thomas had already done this in his famous poem 'Do not go gentle into that good night'), plaiting all the strands with great skill. Ezra Pound said of Ernest Dowson's villanelles that 'the refrains are an emotional fact which the intellect, in the various gyrations of the poem, tries in vain to escape'. This applies to most of the poems in *Brimstone* although at times the form, in such a long sequence, seems under strain. It has to be asked whether Kinsella would have done better by his intensely-felt subjects to vary the forms. At their weakest, they seem mere exercises and rhythms jar, especially when politics obviously enter the lines in a somewhat prosaic, forced manner. Perhaps Louise Glück, newly announced Nobel Prizewinner, puts her finger on a close form such as the villanelle when she says:' I dislike poems that feel too complete, the seal too tight; I dislike being herded into certainty'. This might be too damning here as there is much to admire, especially in Kinsella's honed, mainly lyrical pieces that echo beyond their endings, such as 'Examine Thyself, Singing Honeyeater', 'Moth Lies Down', 'Sunskink Villanellesque', 'The Termites', 'Giant Inflatable Slide Atop a Hill in the Wheatbelt', 'The Frogs' – and the few flaws elsewhere are forgiven when one encounters such musical, memorable villanelles. Kinsella is definitely a man of the land – 'I belong to the faith and feather of flight as searcher for euphony' –

and demonstrates throughout that he knows intimately its flora and fauna. In his finest villanelles, the tone is driven, heartfelt, as towards the end of 'Goading Storms out of a Darkening Field':

Red harvest, charred hills, dry wells filled and sealed.
Sheep on their last legs. Dams crusted over.
Cursing the dry, cursing the bitter yield.

It's tempting when prayers and patience have failed,
Diviners have lost track of ground water.
Goading storms out of a darkening field.
Cursing the dry, cursing the bitter yield.

The traditional themes of change and mortality are to be found in this poem-sequence, and owe something to the French poets Leconte de Lisle and Maurice Rollinat. A number of modern poets have worked with villanelles, exploring the form's capacity to deal with serious themes. These have included William Empson, Theodore Roethke, Sylvia Plath, Roy Fuller and W H Auden. John Kinsella follows in that tradition, at his best bringing lyrical grace to the form's difficulty and intricacies. His themes include drought ('the empty rain-gauge', 'there is no water in the table nor on the surface'), GM crops ('the stock-market in the grainpool', 'grasses eaten away', 'the servants of chemical companies', 'the brash/registered researchers'). His poems record our 'degrees of anxiety' in this regard, how humankind has caused 'the new climate' of disaster and degradation of the planet's resources, 'the dumb debris' of waste, foul air and soil erosion ('red dust coating our lungs') feeling that the bond, the synthesis, with nature is broken. 'Organic harmonies of leaf, stem and root' have gone, he writes, are lost, with 'only emptiness to follow' (he quotes Dante, 'And I have reached a part where no thing gleams'), the 'ancient polity' broken, trees cut down for 'fresh construction of roads' ('fresh' being deliberately ironical). He blames all this on 'the patriarchy,' and on the evils of bureaucracies ('antonyms of nature'). He writes of forest clearings ('fresh bloody ground, open-cut', 'rust of harried earth'), of mass farming ('slaughterhouses'), of cancer-inducing weedkillers ('agri-pastoral rip-off rhetoric'), of 'a whiff of animal death' from floods, fires and storms, Earth no longer our sanctuary, blaming the haters, the warmongers, the capitalists, the spoilers 'who want to burn the world', having lost all 'sacred respect, the shape of the living figure'. The poet fears not only for our children's futures, but for all of the living world's, for moths, fish, frogs, plankton, cicadas, geckoes, termites, anteaters, mice, snails, alpacas, flowers, and everything else, including his beloved butterflies, especially the Brimstone which in its delicacy opposes all the brute forces that are attempting to destroy our world (the other side of 'brimstone' with its sulphurous, satanic implications). Kinsella's poems oppose this violence in 'the life of the spirit' and 'in the silence of prayer'.

The sequence is a timely reminder, in its moral urgency, that nature (which the poet is immersed in) will have its revenge.

> Nothing in me is elevated in making sanctuary
> And the body stress is neither penance nor punishment –
> It's hot late afternoon and I am watering trees
> this is no survivalist act but one of constancy.

Towards the end of the sequence Kinsella strikes a more personal note, such as in 'For my Children'. The children have grown into adults but he misses them in the moving lines:

> My children, I miss you, but don't call you from your tomorrows,
> Don't call you to appear in photos that are self-contained,
> As photos don't tell me anything I can really know
> Though I wonder if for you they make *a sense of things* grow.

The final villanelle, 'Empathy' addresses concern over the Corona virus we are all having to live with:

> Many years ago I was sent a photo of winter mist of cross-season
> mists/ from a poet-friend in Wuhan, now I search it out but can't find
> the past./ I have seen sulphur up on the Peak in Hong Kong in the
> wings of its butterflies.

The delicacy of the butterflies' breath contrasts with the human breath that the virus steals:

> And as the virus flits from breath to breath, as it twists
> Its way into people's lives and afterlives all correlations spread and shift;
> I have seen both brimstone moths and brimstone butterflies –
> An almost pandemic of breath, then no breath whatever its course.

*

Sean O'Brien's latest collection (his tenth) follows on from his last book, *Europa* (2018). *Europa* was concerned with 'massed graves' and 'death of states', with margraves, kings and voivodes, with wars, pogroms and revolutions. *It Says Here* is more involved with England's present depravations and complex recent history :'The world for which the nation fought admits/No Blacks and no dogs and no Irish', 'Aneurin Bevan and Stafford Cripps/and the cold coming of immigrant ships' (note the deliberate echo of T S Eliot in that last phrase), 'the hated State', the physical ravages and mental agonies of old age, exacerbated by the disgraceful treatment of the old in care homes ('the slow disintegrating minds/Grind on'), involved in 'complex economic loathing'.

The most substantial poem in the volume is the long sequence 'Hammersmith' (composed in 'cantos' or chapters) which he calls 'the history of an imagination', where the known and the dreamt 'merge, shift and recombine' in an 'intersection of places', mainly involving personal memories and vignettes of his parents' lives together. I think the poet is unnecessarily humble here, as I find the sequence to be more like a contemporary *Waste Land* than anything else, and a poem which employs similar strategies without recourse to notes. Using the term 'cantos' consciously deflects the reader (one immediately thinks of Pound, for example, or of Tasso, Ariosto, Pope and Byron) but it is the 'exhausted wakefulness' (it is O'Brien's own phrase) of Eliot that one is constantly reminded of ('so much is chaos', 'the harmonies about to shriek themselves apart'). As Eliot reworked a plethora of traditions in his seminal poem, O'Brien reworks traditional English voices (and popular songs and catches) in his, within a contemporary landscape (both in 'Hammersmith' and elsewhere in the book).

It has to be said that the ten Cantos which comprise 'Hammersmith' take most of the reader's attention, and, perhaps, this reviewer would like to suggest, 'Hammersmith' is such a major work that it should have been published on its own. The separate taut, sinewy poems before and after serve as extended prologues and epilogues, and the preliminary poems bear hints of what is to come in the Cantos. For example the lyrical and horrific are mixed, the simile strikingly accurate: 'The roses, hooded from the frost/ Like hangmen, saw that I was lost'. Time, another major theme in 'Hammersmith', has similar treatment in 'Three Songs': 'and yet time haunts itself//and sees you as a ghost'; this pre-empts the different treatments of ghosts in the Cantos. Politics is viewed caustically: 'the secret death of politics... / is, we learn, another name for sex'. And we are all here with the 'monsters' in their 'shallow graves and cellars', monsters that 'swim in blood to be reborn' – 'as if we've dreamed too long to wake', pre-empting the blurring between dream and reality in the Cantos, and also the Cantos' overall dark, bleak vision. O'Brien's sense of rhythm is always faultless, as in the tender poem to a presumably secret lover, 'An Assignation'. Yet even here, in the subject matter, there is a slight twist as the woman in the blue dress (Hardy's 'air-blue gown') raises an empty glass 'As if in toast to no one while I pass/And raise in turn my non-existent hat'. The persona, maybe the poet, is a ghost, with no form.

'Hammersmith', as already implied, is a brilliant tour-de-force, in a class of its own. We are taken on an odyssey, but without the didacticism evident in the journey T S Eliot takes us on in his *Four Quartets*. O'Brien depicts overworlds, underworlds (under the railway and under the river), juxtaposes place names with anonymity, sprinkles his lines with the Classics he updates such as 'Circean perfume', and merges memories into past time – and past time into memory.

Like Eliot, O'Brien makes effective use of repetition in various ways. Refrains, such as 'no place like home since home is nowhere' link to further images of 'home' such as it being 'barely a place', 'no fixed abode', 'false address', emphasising the plight of the poverty-stricken and homeless. Canto III does describe the one home (his) the poet remembers, even though his mother's 'home is the war'. In a very moving section here, O'Brien brings his mother to life as a teacher with a pencil and chalk, and an amateur actress, and he links her life subtly to that of the river:

Now, as her memory goes, I must

Believe it for her: the pan of spuds
Still rippling from the blast, while she
Has lines to learn and books to mark,

An eye to keep on you-know-who.
She walks by the river to get it by heart.
The water is her aide-memoire. *I dare to think*

It can remember her when she is gone.

Named places, too, run throughout the sequence, mainly of various London districts, anchoring it, and accentuating the irony that there is 'no place', 'nowhere'. Even the river that runs through the lines is knowable and unknowable. The Londoners, some of whom are named as Mulligan, Ryan, are immersed in street life, and at times are at a remove from humans we recognise: 'Mechanicals with walkons, at the dancing, at the bar' 'treat the river as themselves'... 'at hand yet out of reach'. 'They build the city; they damn it, dream it, call it theirs' and yet the river remains elusive and answerable to no one until the final Canto X when it is only a momentary different dream river 'at the end of the garden', one the poet 'will never reach'. For in the same Canto it returns, magnified, to being 'the final dark river to nowhere', without even any bedrock. No such spiritual enlightenment emanates here as when 'the fire and the rose are one' at the culmination of *Four Quartets*. O'Brien's existential world has very little reprieve: 'Let books and earth and oily water burn, / Likewise the living and the dead'.

Other repeated images, too, as in *Four Quartets*, are threaded through the Cantos and give them a texture and a cohesiveness – such as a 'suitcase' (the suitcase in Canto II is 'brim-full of the waters of Lethe' and in Canto VIII it is carried by a lodger 'who leaves 'the landing/ With its smell of soup and death'), willows, houseboats, book, 'story', 'poem'; Death itself is like a character: 'Death is scarcely a rumour here. Death is nobody's business' – underlying the taboo on death in Western societies. Death can be a living one: 'you rise from the grave of yourself' and often through the Cantos we are not sure whether the ghosts are ghosts or dead people. In general O'Brien's language is excitingly vivid in its range. It can be lyrical, musical, playful, serious and is sustained by a strong rhythm throughout.

Time too, 'with its 'irreparable betweentimes', is sometimes personified and handled skilfully as O'Brien slips between dream and so-called reality, between 'now' and the post-war period that he summons by extraordinarily accurate concrete images such as 'a pianola/ With its tongue cut out', cardigans, jazz, bombsites, pre-fabs, pinups, the 'revolutionary Olivetti' typewriter which 'Lies beneath its crust of fag-ash / Like a relic of Pompeii', the 'emptiness that smells of brilliantine'. This epoch contrasts to the flyovers, building-sites, girders, bar-rooms, houseboats, tubes – yet everything seems derelict, with the sense of a pervasive loneliness, 'not even solitude but something worse' of the individual.

'Hammersmith' can be read for itself, yet its subtext cleverly consists of a multitude of literary references there for any discerning reader who wishes to unearth them. They add to the density and majesty of the work. For example: here is Eliot himself in 'raggedy scuttlers down on the slime-bed' (one thinks of 'Prufrock'), Lloyds Bank (where Eliot worked), Edmund Spenser (both in the epigraph to the poem, from *The Faerie Queen*, and in mention of 'the silver-black Thames' – Eliot himself quotes Spenser in 'The Fire Sermon' section of *The Waste Land*, 'Sweet Thames, run softly, till I end my song'). Virgil is there (in 'slow fields of Hades'), Philip Larkin (in 'And past the door the stairs go up… To a final room for rent that shows', and in 'the lodger with a single suitcase'. Larkin's poem 'Church Going' can also be heard in the phrases 'An empty sepulchre' and 'the grave's aphasia'. Basil Bunting is there (from *Briggflatts*) in 'From the streets where

133

the gasping buses grind on', and W.H. Auden in 'What might have been had England kept the faith' (O'Brien is referring to Brexit angst here) and 'the clerks are sneaking off and there are hangmen at the gate' (an echo here also of 'hangmen, hangmen everywhere' from *Europa*). Auden can also be heard in the phrase 'As you lay sleepless in my arms', as is Milton in 'The leering creatures spit for England but/ Since time is money will not stand and wait'. Pound is to be found (his 'prose kinema' from *Hugh Selwyn Mauberley*) in 'A private cinema of thirst and failure/With the same thing always showing' (with an echo also of Prufrock's 'As if a magic lantern threw nerves in patterns on a screen'). Dante's *Inferno* (which O'Brien has translated) can be heard in 'There lies a mouth forever opening/To discharge a stream of language wedded/to the slur and swallow of the water'. There are oblique references to Evelyn Waugh and Harold Macmillan ('to decline and fall, to a wind of change'), Robert Frost ('the way through the woods') and to D.H. Lawrence ('the bride and the gamekeeper'). Shakespeare crops up from time to time, in 'that blessed plot' (an allotment now, and not so blessed), in Fortinbras' 'iron eloquence', and in the cultural clash between Caliban and Ariel (with possible allusions to Auden's 'The Sea and the Mirror' and to Robert Browning's 'Caliban upon Setebos'). Keith Douglas is there in 'But oh forget me not, forget me not', Wittgenstein in 'knowing that all this is merely the case', and Geoffrey Hill in 'dying a little faster every day' — one thinks of Hill's 'hurtling to oblivion'. In fact, the cover to O'Brien's book is a detail from *A House Collapsing on Two Firemen, Shoe Lane, London* by Leonard Rosoman, which also featured in Hill's *The Book of Baruch by the Gnostic Justin* in 2019: 'Len Rosoman in Shoe Lane./Write on that if you can./ One man pressed flat as a skate,/ even his tin hat'. Maybe O'Brien was tempted by the challenge). There are also direct mentions of Josephine Tey, Gustav Holst, Charles Baudelaire (his nightmarish cityscapes and Walter Benjamin's essay on his modernist influence), J.R.R. Tolkien, C.S. Lewis, Wallace Stevens, Theodore Roethke, Yeats, Chaucer, Dryden, John Berryman and James Wright.

A character in 'Hammersmith', Mulligan, is an amalgam of Samuel Beckett's Molloy and Murphy, wandering in a 'city/mined with unexploded ordnance//Sunk among the bones in flooded graves'. Phrases such as 'the final dark river to nowhere', 'there is no bedrock to be found', 'what we stand for must be nothingness', 'Here there is nowhere. Here is no stay', 'There was a gate, but nobody alas/Has found it', 'God is not... He's just not', reinforce the Beckettian background. So it is O'Brien teases us consciously with literary references as Eliot did in his work, highlighting at the same time contemporary cant and political jargon ('we neither affirm or deny', 'the secret death of politics' in an age of 'wonks and spads and black ops cybermen').

'Hammersmith' then is a sort of 'palace of varieties' (the phrase is O'Brien's own, with maybe a nod towards The Hammersmith Palais). There are references to popular music hall and television performers such as Max Bygraves and Mike and Bernie Winters. The poem reads at times like an early centennial celebration of, or homage to, Eliot's great poem of 1922. The same element of pastiche is certainly at work there.

O'Brien also dwells on his own aging in the volume, still practising what he sees as 'the dying art' of poetry (in *Europa* it was 'art is all there is and/ and might not be enough'), on his mother teaching through the Blitz, as we have already seen, on his parents' courtship in 'a world of fags and Guinness', his father 'a ghost/who cannot find his level of damnation'. We have vignettes of O'Brien's own memories of radio, early television shows, and demob suits, 'a stench of gas and sewage//In the deserted street', the bombed-out city, the dangers of the imagination, the temptation to suicide, and snapshots of 'lost afternoons' ('drowned in the mirror of the dim afternoon') as a student. In a collection mainly taken up with the brutal and the banal, the poet struggles through depression to find some hope in the end: 'But let me remember the possible days,/ The river, where the garden ends//And those I lost are walking still', poetry 'a charm against the dark'.

O'Brien's poetry confronts a world in which words no longer 'bear scrutiny' and where they are stripped of meaning and truth. His poetry opposes that trend by restoring the noble traditions of English (and American) literature, exposing also at the same time the shamelessness of contemporary politics. Like John Kinsella his work demonstrates that poetry can serve as a polemic, a public warning, against degradation and barbarism. He has faith in the power of the Imagination to break through what he calls 'the marble wing of madness'.

*

Patricia McCarthy's *Whose hand would you like to hold* is a shorter work than John Kinsella's and Sean O'Brien's, but is equally compelling, breaking away as it does from the constraint of the lyric to narrate a multi-faceted story overlaid by the fear, anxiety and grief of the Covid-19 pandemic. It is a voice for our time, shedding light on our shared humanity and on the value of relationships and connections, also on the faithful cyclical patterns of nature that innocently continue despite man's blunderings. It rises above this time in the power of its details akin to Wordsworth's 'spots of time' and in this way it illuminates and says more, through metaphor, about our human condition than any straight take on the pandemic. McCarthy has a broad story to tell from unique angles, and each poem, in a way, like in her previous collections, *Rodin's Shadow*, *Horses Between Our Legs*, *Letters to Akhmatova*, *Trodden Before* and *Rockabye*, has its own story. It is the force of the saying and the strength of the metaphor that give the poetry its power. All the poems, which comprise really one long poem, are interlocked, interrelated with a natural rhythm to the voice which, despite the raw nature of the subject, maintains lyrical grace.

Like *Brimstone* and *It Says Here*, McCarthy's poem-sequence is extremely relevant, the story detailed, convincing and haunting, with a drive to telling the truth about our present devastation, as well as commemorating all those who have 'gone before in plagues'. In this manner, she locates the current crisis within the context of a broader, longer history, including that of other pandemics. This helps us to put into perspective our present situation – through the focus of what happened then.

In the Prologue she introduces the 'writing' theme via the Bronte sisters who were differently locked down in their own world, with their own invented stories from *Angria*, *Glass Town* and Charlotte's *Roe Head* journals: 'Time to sit as the Brontes did,/ the wind rattling its commentary// to windows and doors – as if ghosts/ of loved ones crave re-entry'. This reference is to Emily's ghost that shouts to Heathcliff through the window of Wuthering Heights to let her in. And indeed, Emily seems to be the mentor here to encourage all who start to write when locked up indoors: 'Emily's fierce faithful dog, Keeper,/ on guard in your psyches, will escort you// over your minds' wildest moors' and Emily herself , undergoing with her sisters and brother, the endemic of Tuberculosis from which, turn by turn, they all went into the 'decline' and eventually died, will 'scribble', with your own secrets 'her secrets, fast as she can'. This presumably links to McCarthy writing her sequence in one great flow, quickly and surely in the altered claustral time.

The Black Death too is paralleled to the present pandemic: 'This cottage has known it before;/its long cold room with its musty air/ offered as a mortuary, sin-eaters chanting outside and glorified bodies/ inside souls escaping, soot-coated/ up wide chimney breasts'… The half-rhyming end couplet stresses there are 'Lessons to learn from shut doors/ about the blackest Black Death's cure', the half-rhyme implying a speck of hope, here, as elsewhere, with the form of the poem speaking in a subtext.

In the following poem a ratcatcher 'appears through cob walls' with his specialised knowledge of rats who 'jump not at his throat but at the light – / on the lookout for Pied Pipers who will believe//they can lead children over their own runs/ and scrapes into underground caves/ to be petted for their intelligence and fur'. However, the persona or poet, is 'Unnerved by his eyes', and doesn't 'tell of skeletons/ haunting the stair'. The poem begins and ends with a line from the nursery rhyme 'Ring of roses' which of course was written in the Black Death, 'We all fall down' referring to all the victims falling down dead.

The theme of children is continued in McCarthy's coverage of the polio epidemic in England in the 1950s. Here the detail brings the poem alive and it is further strengthened by her personal experience. She recalls 'tiny faces peering, as if from Advent calendars,//from communal iron lungs'. The image is exact and all the more harrowing as it is clothed in the lyrical, as are the 'tiny coffins that glisten//in the sun, ready, it seems to put on merry-go-rounds,/ not to sink into the soil'. The childhood casualties of these older pandemics serve to warn those in the current pandemic who believe it is only the old who are affected. In this poem there is a subtle, hardly noticeable rhyme scheme, each stanza of four lines having the first and third line rhyming alternately with the third and fourth lines. The rhyme scheme breaks down when the child (the poet herself) nearly dies, then resumes again while 'Outside, playmates hide behind a wall of sweet peas,/ the cricket field's three-legged races, the arrows// chalked on winding lanes where we play Tracking/ old Will's pigs, the lily ponds… are still there./ So is the polio'.

In the third poem of the sequence 'Holy week, our childhood voices singing/ Gregorian chant faroff' is recalled but it seems that the Faith has long since been lost: 'Long have we swapped/ naves for woodland paths, treading in imprints of a man who shouldered everyone// on his way to the cross'.

Where 'ash dieback/ matches the dieback of people', in our mainly Godless society, maybe, the poet implies, we need more than ever now to 'hear/ the tapping of nails into flesh and wood'. Again in the poem about her newly-widowed sister in France, where mainly in every two verses the second lines rhyme, (just as she wants to rhyme with her sister and take her back to their childhood haunts in this country):

You could hear again the first cuckoo, shyer
and rarer now than the ones we used to hear
and treasure all year-round in cuckoo clocks.

The poet would like to pick bluebells again as in their childhood, 'their liquid stems that used to fill/ the baskets on our fairy bikes, our chanted spells/ accompanied by the rattles of their chains//all the way home.' Then, towards the end of the sequence, there is a fine elegy concerning future generations , suggesting to all parents/grandparents how, 'in years to come', they will remind their children about how life was, a world they will, scarily, never have known, 'how daffodils... were trumpets played by angels// how spiders' webs caught in the sun at dawn/ had to unravel their filigree mandalas to string violins'. The next poem, 'Ice Child', branches out to tackle the climate crisis and social disturbances 'plagues, mass shootings, famines, knives/ with no trekking routes, no boats/ over ice floes for rescue'. The poet makes a plea: 'Stay without flesh, child of our time'. For

The price of skin is vulnerability,
alienation...

She ends the poem with an impassioned plea: 'May the silence/ in your heart keep the song inside you'.

There are love poems here: for humans in general such as the less privileged confined to tiny flats and tenements who only have window-ledges to lean on to get outside, yet when cellists and violinists 'play from rooftops': 'In a few soaring seconds the have-nots/ become the haves, crescendos, grace notes/ chords unifying every breath'. Compassion is woven into sonnets that lay bare, and box in, what graphically happens, for those suffering from escalated domestic violence; for commuters now 'in the cocoon of furloughed days', for the bereaved, for those with dementia in care homes: 'the forgotten ones who have forgotten themselves'. She also recollects her mother's days as a 'key worker' nursing 'victims/of cholera, smallpox, leprosy, with no masks,/goggles or special gowns, simply//a starched white uniform', and she goes on to imagine her own mother, still alive, in a care home. The poet, her daughter, dabs 'rouge on her high cheekbones', buys her 'favourite Chanel lipstick'. The details bring the mother alive – and the daughter who plays the honkytonk piano in the home, forgetting her shyness in order to entertain the residents Other love poems are there, often with something secretive, perhaps forbidden about them induced by heightened emotion in the pandemic, haunted by wished-for, wasted, or acclaimed lovers who might never be seen again, by last chances and chances not taken. Literary references, classical allusions and other religions than Christianity, including Eastern religions, are thrown into the mix. And birds' 'swoopings, soarings' contrast with our limited freedom; there are pink, blue and ordinary moons, 'lamb-dancing fields', weddings that can't happen with 'ghosts of all the brides/ who unstitched their gowns' and no grooms, a mare who has lost her beloved horse companion and whose instinct enables her to cope with the bereavement: 'you lay where/ her sweet body was dragged into the field.// You roll there still for companionship/ when you have only the summer sheep// and the wind mounting you in your season' – a whole cosmos constructed through the poet's vision. Not all is despair despite the look that is 'terrible' on the faces of Rilke's pagan angels in the Epilogue, for 'the heart/ has its guardians, mellow-tongued, whatever the country' and if we all 'tread carefully', we will see 'even the wayward sink into tenderness'.

The strength of McCarthy's sequence lies in its avoidance of the confessional mode, and her ability in composing an objective, sustained narrative. There is a grace and clarity to her writing which is unusual in this day and age, and what I like most is her celebration of human courage, dignity and composure. The tone throughout the sequence is quiet and humane, avoiding any note of cynicism or despair. These are qualities I would argue that are in short supply these days, and are therefore the more to be cherished and respected.

All three books reviewed here emphasise the need for such a wake up call, and we are lucky to have such voices to listen to. Patricia McCarthy calls it 'the special balm' of literature, and we'd all be lost without it.

Photographs: Will Stone, from a series of 'Fragmented Remembrance' portraits from Belgian cemeteries which have weathered and suffered damage through time and the elements and thus are transmogrified into something else... powerful existential symbols of loss, forgetting, time, the meaning of perpetuity.

CHOSEN YOUNG BROADSHEET POETS

Natalie Crick (29 years, Newcastle) has poems published in *Stand, Poetry Salzburg Review, The Moth, Banshee* and *New Welsh Review*. She is studying for an MPhil in Creative Writing at Newcastle University. Natalie's poetry has been commended in various competitions, including The Anthony Cronin International Poetry Award 2018, The Hippocrates Open Awards for Poetry and Medicine 2019 and The Verve Poetry Festival Competition 2020. She was awarded second prize in The Newcastle Poetry Competition 2020.

Glentrool

For the walls she painted all the same:
lilac to match her jumper and her ceilings.

For her high kicks and cartwheels
on the living room carpet.

For the *Birds* powdered custard, deliciously
thick with milk and a shiny skin. We ate it
late at night after Grandad's special hotpot.

For the space under the floorboards
where she hid secrets in balls of wool,
for fear we would steal them.

For the long winter walks with Mamie
through wet cobbled streets
until the skies grew dark.

For the rooms filled with loud laughter,
which would fade, but reappear
in glorious, unexpected moments.

For the corners pinned with lists of names
she knew she would forget.

For the garden games we played; hide and seek,
hunting for earwigs to drown, brewing potions
in the shed from herbs and food colouring.

For the later years when she left *Glentrool*
and ran away, tired of the stillness.
Sometimes she got lost.

For *Glentrool*, the little bungalow in Sunderland,
far from the Galloway Hills. Memories
never forgotten, a place to visit to forget.

Saddleworth

The searchers are coming out of the woods
with bramble bruises,
eyes ready, jaws set.
They're holding hands in long chains,
they're murmuring the sermons of our fathers,
they're murmuring the names:
'Pauline, John, Lesley'.

The searchers are sheep entranced
across Saddleworth. The medicine sky
is the autumnal grey of a lone wren;
neither night nor day, dark nor light,
neither slumberous nor waking.
⁃ They get as far as they can, but
not too far to fall, half-lost.

Clouds sail astray, stained with sunset and
the searchers wander home to broken sleep.
In my dream, the soft chimes of the bell
around Keith's neck toll as he stirs.
'Here I am. Here I am'. He wanders to Shiny Brook,
and we find him. Singing to a robin,
we find him.

But today more searchers are coming out of the woods.
They're shifting snow and raking leaves.
They're searching for Keith with his light brown hair.
Mist roves from the purples in the grass
and the lamps fade in heaven again.
Silently searchers mourn in the marshes:
'Keith, Keith'

for there will be a day when he will waft home
asleep forever with the flowered souls.
At night the searchers wait
with their knives where the grasses grow tall.
It smells like rain and
I wish I had a prayer and a gun, my love,
I wish I had a prayer and a gun.

The Hurrier

The Hurrier calls me 'bastard'
and 'naughty boy'. I blush red
as the Hurrier's bedroom curtains.

She's there
riding her fairy bike,
legs shot down, arms out.

The Hurrier bedevils me
in quiet clothes of grey,
waving her short knobby stick.

Her skirt blows across her thighs.
The wind messes her thinning hair
all upset and hurdy gurdy.

She's there
under the spring insect moon.
The stable clock rattles

when she hurries past.
I'm there when she rides by
the brothel and the butcher's shop.

On the sports field, I sink into
the tang of cut grass and
try to look away but

my eyes lock into her devil-
may-care smile. My finger
rings her bell for a charm.

Genevieve Stevens lives in London with her husband and two children. Recent work has appeared in *PN Review, The Moth, Acumen, Agenda, Sentinel* and *Wild Court*. Stevens also writes reviews for *Review31, Agenda, Poetry School* and *Caught by the River*. She will shortly begin a practice-based poetry Ph.D at Royal Holloway University.
On page 124 she reviews Laura Scott.

And also with you

Because her hair came loose just as she turned
he could not help but think of jasmine –
how fallen tendrils must be taught to loop the wire
and fan for light and O how his wife used to help
the climbers climb – even pulling the necks of weeds
she would assert an integrity of purpose and all this while
the woman with the wayward curls is thinking only
how strange it is to find no conflict between faith
in spring's return and her suspicion that life
ends with death, and that is all.

Gossipers on the South Western

You would think they had nothing to say,
the way they hand it to each other –
crêpe paper, string, a gift the size of two
average hands –

Pass.

     Pass back.

And with each tilt of conversation it does not grow,
or gain weight, or reveal itself to be the answer.
But how they guard it! Stashing it under coats and bags
when the attendant comes, who clears his throat to say
nothing as he stubs their day returns. Only then,
when he's far enough away do they raise it up again –
one woman passing so the other can receive
the swish of the crepe, the tangled promise of the string.

NOTES FOR BROADSHEET POETS

An interview with Peter Weltner

P McC: Peter what made you start to write poetry?

PW: I started to read poetry very young, mostly poems published in anthologies meant for children given me by relatives. *Silver Pennies* was one of them. I was brought up Lutheran and served as an altar boy for several years. I liked listening to passages read from the bible as an essential part of the service, especially the psalms for their music, whether read or sung. In my early teens, I discovered Matthiessen's *Oxford Anthology of American Poetry*. That's where I first found Eliot, Hart Crane, Ezra Pound, and so many other poets I've continued to read throughout my life. My teen years were also an extraordinary time for little magazines; the *Evergreen Review* was one I recall in particular which I bought at a news and magazine shop down the street from our Church that was open after noon on Sundays as well as magazines championing the recent American painting, mostly out of New York, that I had seen there, *Art News* and *Arts*. I wasn't much good, but I fancied myself a painter at the time. A lot of the reviews in both those magazines were a sort of poetry in themselves. But it was reading two writers otherwise almost each other's opposites, Gertrude Stein and Dylan Thomas, that got me attempting my very bad imitations of both. Those were my first poems, fortunately long forgotten. In college, I came under the greater sway of Eliot and Pound. The selections from Pound I first discovered in Matthiessen's anthology offered a music like none I had ever heard before. Finally, Caedmon records had published two LP discs of contemporary poets reading from their work. Conrad Aiken's reading of his *Tetélestai* still sounds in my head. All these and more were instigations.

P McC: Were you encouraged to write (and learn) poetry when at high school?

PW: My high school published a literary magazine. There was also an organization devoted to student writing, *Quill and Scroll*. I was active in it, designing covers and writing both poems and stories for it. I also was fortunate to have good English teachers who obviously really loved poetry. I remember, for example, Sara Mims reading Bryant's 'Thanatopsis' aloud to us and weeping through the poem's last lines. Yes, it was sentimental. But poetry to her and to my even finer teacher, Peggy Anne Joyner, really mattered to them. We read extensively in the British and American traditions. Of course, it was at Hamilton College that I really learned how to read. The teachers there were influenced by the New Criticism, but in a loose and non-dogmatic way. I still think it is the best way to read so long as one embraces a lot else as well.

P McC: Did you have any particular mentors who encouraged you on your poetic journey?

PW: Not mentors in poetry, but in painting, though I would not make the distinction strict. The later fifties in the US were an extraordinary time for art. Black Mountain was not far from where I grew up, and the Woman's College of the University of North Carolina in Greensboro had an exceptionally fine and innovative arts program. Through my painting, I got to know a lot of the artists in the area, most of them at least a decade or so older than I was. Gerald Coble was the most important. He is still alive and still makes wonderful work. He became my teacher for a year. We talked about everything and listened to a lot of music together. One of the things he was teaching me was what it meant to be serious about any art. Randall Jarrell taught at WC. I was a friend of his step-daughter. Through her, I got to know him and Mary a little. Just about everything he said has stayed with me. Our one disagreement was about Rothko. I cherish that.

P McC: I notice in your very modest short biography at the end of your wonderful book of poems *Bird and Tree/In Place* (Marrowstone Press), you taught English Renaissance poetry and prose and modern and contemporary British, Irish and American fiction and poetry at San Francisco State university for thirty seven years. That alone is quite a mammoth achievement over such a broad span. First of all, do you think the study of literature encourages and even inspires students to tap into their own creative writing processes? Or does it put them off? And secondly, would you encourage a potential young poet to study poetry as literature rather than enrolling on a Creative Writing course, often leading to a degree? What do you think of the latter fashion for Creative Writing Bachelor, Masters and even PhD degrees?

PW: While I taught there, San Francisco State had a large and influential Creative Writing Department that offered both a BA and an MA. Originally, it and the English Department were one department. The split occurred shortly after I arrived on campus. Among the writers in Creative Writing then or a bit earlier were Wright Morris, Kay Boyle, Robert Creeley, John Logan, Robert Duncan, Leo Litwak, William Dickey, Stan Rice, Jack

Gilbert, and Mark Linenthal. The creative writing students were required to take a certain number of courses in English Literature. I think that makes for a very good balance. Many, maybe most of my best students were those working for a degree in Creative Writing. Its presence in my life was very important to my own work, both as a teacher and a writer. Which was more important to its students? That would depend on the student-writer. I never took any creative writing classes anywhere. If I had to choose, I would advise any aspiring writer to read as much as she or he can from as many different languages and traditions as possible. I will add, though, that I have never quite understood what good the Creative Writing workshops offer.

P McC: This leads to the question: do you think it right to make a student of Creative Writing think their whole aim is to be published?

PW: No. I wrote fiction and some poetry for twenty years before I published any of it. My first book appeared when I was 47. I do not think of writing as a career, perhaps because I had my teaching, but as a vocation. I mean that word in a religious sense. I do not want to idealize writing, or any art, so much that the practical parts of it are ignored. But I do think one of the ways I might disagree with a good deal of the poetry world today is the emphasis it places on various sorts of success which smack, like it or not, of values which the arts might do better opposing. How, I do not know. I also worry a lot about the conformity of so much recent poetry published in the US, especially of the ideological sort. It is a poetry that knows what it is going to say long before it says it. That is one meaning of rhetoric, it seems to me. A formal poem of any sort has trouble getting published in the US these days, as do poems which do not consider themselves overtly, purposefully political.

I think poetry can be that, but it should also be a whole lot more, the totality of what it means to be human, for one. And it should always leave room for the uncertain, for the unsaid, for mystery and strangeness and wonder, to be more than a bit wide-eyed about it.

P McC: You seem to write your life out in your corpus of poems and yet your poems are not confessional, nor are they limited to an over-insistence on the first person 'I'. What do you think of poets writing autobiographical poems, eg I love the way you confide how, when your mother died 'I dreamed/ of her alive every night for weeks, for months' (the same thing happened to me when my father died)… And what do you think of what some see as the eternal problem of the 'I' in poetry?

PW: What I make of the 'I' in poetry depends, of course, on the poem. What I would try to discover through reading it is how the poem uses it. I think nearly everything I have written tells, in one way or another, a story, whether explicitly or implicitly. It might be a mistake ever to read any poem in which 'I' appears, even those that present themselves as confessional or transparently personal, as autobiographical in any strict sense, that is in any merely factual way, because the act of writing itself creates another 'I' which both is and is not the 'I' of the writer.

For me, this means something different from the idea of the poem as personally confessional or the notion of the poem as a persona or mask for the poet since even the most intentionally personal poems are the work of a story teller, and every storyteller knows, or intuits somehow, that the story he or she might have intended to write changes in the writing of it into something different from oneself, into something more than oneself, something, one hopes, more meaningful and deeper.

Of course, some 'I's in poems are complete fictions, narrative creations. Others are obvious attempts at the realization of someone else's voice altogether, someone whom one knows or loves or who is historical or mythic and so on.

What your question makes me wonder about is, when those sorts of poems I just mentioned are not what one is talking about, where does the line between the personal and the persona of a poem in which some 'I' speaks get drawn. I guess my answer would be: it can't be drawn. One can't know. Nor should one want to know because that impossibility is part of the way in which the writing and reading of poetry is a deepening of life, of all lives, those of its poet and those of its readers.

The biography of the poet is transformed by the poem into the biography of the poem. The details of the writer's life found in it may or may not conform to the facts of that life. What happens, though, is that in the writing of the poem those facts change into the larger pattern of images and rhythms and shapes, and all the rest of it, that make up the poem itself.

We say, occasionally too easily, poems might change your life, whether of the reader or writer. Well, the 'I' who wrote the poem is inevitably changed into the 'I' of the poem. So a certain sort of myth making, of transcendence, is both unavoidable and essential. I hope that does not sound pretentious. It seems to me true even of the simplest, seemingly most transparent poems of William Carlos Williams, say, or the later work of Carl Rakosi where it appears a life is merely being recorded, almost journalistically. That that is not so is why such poems are in fact poems and not diaries. And surely the Robert Lowell of *Life Studies* or the Sylvia Plath of *Ariel* are fictions, the transformation of the biographical self into the mythic self, if by the people found in myths we mean those who bear in their selves, their I's, implications beyond the personal.

P McC: Visual art and many artists are important to you; indeed, you yourself paint with words. I also love your collaborations with the powerfully inspiring Galen Garwood. Music, too (eg the music of your voice and its lines) and many composers obviously inspire you and are even part of you. What do you think of poetry's relation to other art forms?

PW: I guess that the briefest answer would be that I hope they might be nearly inextricably close. It is hard for me to imagine a poetry without some relationship with music, whatever sort of music it might be. Mine tends toward classical, but others might find it more in pop music or folk music or jazz or rap, it does not matter so long as it attunes one's ear to hear better and more assuredly the music in poems, the specific sounds of the poems one wishes to write or to read. I don't mean just the rhythms. I would wish, in the musical patterns, to include harmony, consonances and dissonances, and all the rest of it, including melodies and tunes, not just the beat. I like poems best that seem to sing while at the same time keeping close to a speaking voice, a voice speaking as it might, however heightened, in a conversation or in dialogue.

When I was seventeen, I saw at New York's Museum of Modern Art, an exhibit of what was then called The New American Painting. I had been going to museums, often with my parents or friends, for years. I had seen work that has ever since stayed with me. But that show changed my life for it gave me a sense, better said, an experience of how the image, even the 'abstract' image, could point to realities beyond itself. Later, I would come to understand that that experience is true of all important art. But that experience is the one that first converted me. The artist Gerald Coble, whom I met the same year, showed me even more clearly what such an experience meant in the making of art. I myself failed as a painter (and even worse, earlier, as a violin and oboe player. Excruciatingly bad.) He taught me that what most matters in a painting is what it points to.

I believe all the arts are bound together. The differences among them are a matter of emphases, what music can stress that poetry cannot so purely, and painting what poetry cannot so immediately, and dancing what poetry cannot so physically, and so forth. Yet poetry nonetheless can also be pure, immediate, physical and all the other things one might consider to define some other art form. It is a matter of attuning one's senses, soul, intelligence and all the rest of it to what is made manifest and possible through all the arts as one participates in any one of them. And the subsequent effort in the making of it to keep it, whether dance or music or painting or poem, as simple and direct as possible, with little or no striving after effects or blatant implications and resemblances. I hope this does not sound presumptuous or overbearing as I fear it might.

When I was still teaching, whether Renaissance drama or Faulkner or contemporary poetry, the first minutes of every class were devoted to my students' reading aloud from the play, novel, or poem before us, the physical presence of the words made present before any attempt we might make to interpret them. I wanted them, if possible, to sense and to feel the words in their bodies as much as possible first. It is amazing to hear how some prose, for example portions of the Quentin section of *The Sound and the Fury*, when read aloud in a group or even just to oneself seems to dance.

P McC: You don't sound presumptuous at all. Far from it. Now, let's see... Much of your poetry seems to rely on memory which, in turn, links to time. Can you comment on this?

PW: Language itself is a force of memory, isn't it? Doesn't every word include in its meaning the presence of the past? I don't just mean its etymology, but the history, as much as one knows it, of its usage, then and now. I don't understand how there can be art without memory, for good or for ill. The ideal some writers seem to strive for of an art freed from the past strikes me as incomprehensible. We are at least two presences more than ourself: the past and the place we find ourselves in and through, thrown there or not, wanting to be there or not.

No moment in history, our own very much included, is free from fault or guilt, abuse and cruelty. Art is a way to remember that allows us all, however doomed to failure it is, to recognize that moral fact while at the same time acknowledging that some of the past must be rejected and some must be saved. Forgetfulness of the past or the pasts we have inherited is the greatest human ethical danger. If to remember is a recognition, a realization, of how the past has wounded us, it is also an acknowledgement of what parts of it must be saved if we are to save ourselves. That is a fundamental beginning for something like an ethics of poetry.

Some poets, a while back – I am thinking of one of The Language Poets here in SF in the early eighties whose meetings at 80 Langton Street I occasionally attended – struggled for a pure language scrubbed of the past for the purposes of an almost utopian vision, both of society and language itself. Some such aspiration remains at large in the world of the arts even still.

The danger of that and other assaults upon the past is that memory, even when it might overwhelm one, remains the only way to save oneself from its excesses. But memory is also an expressive force of passionate feelings, too, especially those erotic ones that make possible, in words at least, the return of what's been lost, especially the loss of those you have loved, whether through death or separation or the severing workings of time's malice in other ways.

The memories that mean the most to me, may in the end mean all to me, are like those that other writers have summoned far better than I am able to do, mostly about love. Nearly all the best poems born from memory are love poems. I don't wish to imply that the lover is always absent. Far from it. For to love is also to remember – even as one wakes up in the morning beside him or her still soundly sleeping – all you have felt and known and experienced with this man or woman, of what their very presence in its immediacy evokes of the past and places and all the other moments you have shared together, however long ago it happened.

Memory, of course, is always the presence of the past, in a love poem perhaps of everything you and he or she have ever been and meant together, whether for one night only or thirty five years. For it is in the intensity of the deepest feelings of love or a great passion that one feels most the enormity of all that is missing. It matters, of course it matters, whether the loved one is present or not, alive or not, with you or elsewhere. But to you, not to the poem in which love and memory are much the same thing.

P McC: You say somewhere 'All poetry is repetition'. Is this linked to your interest in the Classics?

PW: Yes, in part. My interest in classics began in high school when I read Latin with a wonderful teacher, Mary Madlin, for several years. I continued that study in college, as a side to my major, and, since my dissertation on John Lyly's plays was in English Renaissance drama, it grew in grad school as well. In my early years teaching at SFState, I often taught a course that included a lot of Greek and Roman writing, in translation of course. But my real interest in the classical past goes deeper than that, one I won't elaborate upon here. It has to do with an abiding obsession with the tension between the classical tragic sense and that of Christianity in the iconography of the cross. It is about, god help us, trying to figure out, hopeless as it is, some meaning to suffering.

In any case, a lot of the present I see manifest in the classical past. My poems that offer classical themes are, of course, really about the present anyway. Forrest Gander once joked to me, about one of my books, that he did not know so many Romans had settled on Point Reyes.

About repetition. 'All' undoubtedly overstates. What I mean is something like this. Years ago, I saw a documentary about Ezra Pound from late in his life. I hope I am remembering this correctly. If not, I will let it stand anyway. He was wearing around his neck and over one shoulder down his chest a scarf on which had been sewn or somehow inscribed in Chinese three words he translated as Sun Sun Again. Pound said that he always wore it and intimated that what those three words, that bit of calligraphy, meant: Make It New.

To make new for Pound was not to reject the past, but to repeat it as a returning of it. The sun each times it arises is the same sun, we say, while it is also of course a different one, at the least a day older. From the point of us, human beings, one never sees the same sunrise, of course. It is and should be always new to us, each day's rising. The same sun, if we are lucky, rises again and again. It repeats itself, yes, but it and we are also constantly changing.

It is a bit like, if only slightly so, a theme in music that stays the same underlying theme while going through its musical changes during the duration of the piece.

I think something like that is often true of poetry. Each poem is new. But each new poem is and must be – it cannot be avoided, even if one wanted to try to do so – a repetition of one kind or another: of form, music, sense, language, image, on and on. In this way it resembles, though only resembles, what Eliot was speaking about when he wrote of the intersection of the timeless with time. I think Pound meant something of the same sort when he first insisted on poetry's making it new, though I believe as well that exhortation has long been misunderstood.

To make new means, I'm suggesting, to express how the old or the past or a memory shines through that new thing. It is a way of recollecting, in several senses, the enduring: one saw that same sun rise yesterday, you remember that, but how differently it rises today. Poetry might be, I guess I am trying to say, a manifestation of what endures through change. In poems, it may simply be the resemblances of the words used and how they echo earlier words and music. I suggest this only as a possible example.

None of what I am saying here might be true of all poetry. Undoubtedly it is not. So 'all' is wrong. But it surely haunts my own and the work of a lot of other writers, to the good of it, I hope, this call of the past, whether you are conscious of it or not or of some 'otherness' beyond you more enduring than you alone could ever hope to be. Maybe this offers a glimpse of what I mean by 'repetition.' Harold Bloom famously invented the phrase 'the anxiety of influence'. I would reject that phrase for 'the necessity of influence', for its grace and generosity and inspirations, the kind of repetition that is, in art, a revival and revivification.

P McC: What advice would you give to a young person wanting to become an established poet?

PW: I am lousy at giving advice. I would say first not to worry about becoming "established". I would say second write because you must, because your life in some way depends upon it, not for any other reason. Let the rest of it find its way, if it will.

P McC: Here you chime in with what Rilke says in his *Letters to a Young Poet*.

Have you had any difficulties or blocks in becoming a celebrated, known poet?

PW: Since I am certainly not celebrated and hardly known except by a small group of loyal readers, I am really not one to answer this question. What I have been given, for which I am most grateful, is several publishers who have published my work over and over no matter the sales. The only books of mine that broke two thousand in sales were a collection of stories, *The Risk of His Music*, and a novel, *How the Body Prays*, both published by Graywolf in the '90s. They were also nationally reviewed. That has not happened with the poetry. But the publishing world has changed in many ways since then in any case, in some ways to the good. Small presses are ever more important.

P McC: What is your personal writing process? For example, do you write poetry every day or only when it is pressed out of you?

PW: I write almost every day and toss out a lot of it. I live by the Pacific, just a few doors west, and walk our dog by it nearly every morning, quite early, often while it is still dark. That's where and how a poem will start – lines, a rhythm, something of both coming into my head. The ocean is all over the place in my work these last twenty years.

P McC: Regarding the whole poetry scene nowadays both here and in the US, don't you think that to get your work out there, you need to be a self publicist, and this does not necessarily tally with a sensitive, possibly shy would-be poet?

PW: I am too old to be interested or have any place in a scene of any sort. I did enjoy certain scenes when I was younger here in SF, the group that published Five Fingers Books and Review, for one, the Language poets at 80

Langton Street, though I did not take to their poetics, the people around and friendly with Robert Duncan, for another. I think young or younger writers can find a lot of comfort and inspiration in those sorts of groupings. They can also, deleteriously, sometimes encourage certain doctrinaire views. I think serious poetry must allow for a lot of silence and solitude, too. Some of the shyest poets, Emily Dickinson for one, have been among our best.

P McC: As you say, you also write prose. In fact, you have published twenty books or chapbooks of fiction or poetry. What is the main difference between your prose and your poetry?

PW: Not as much as one might think. I wrote my stories and novels much as I write poems, guided by the ear, the rhythms and sounds of the words. Poetry, it has been said, is attention intensified into music. The same for me is true of a story or a novel. Furthermore, many of my poems have a narrative drive to them; I am often still telling stories in poems.

Two books of mine, little read, which Marrowstone published, *The Return of What's Been Lost* and *Antiquary*, include both stories and poems interspersed to show how they do belong together, are intimate with one another, exist in dialogue together.

P McC: Is there anything else you would like to say to a budding poet?

PW: Write because you have to, because your life would not be possible without it. Read as much as you can from as many different traditions as you can. Learn as much as you can about as many different ideas and ways of thinking as you can. Think of writing as a way of finding what you did not know already before you wrote it.

P McC: What inspires you?

PW: Let me be pretentious, even more so than I have been thus far, I reckon. What inspires me are the joys and sorrows of life, the tragedies and the comedies of it, the continuing search for an ever more elusive sense of the meanings of it all, the problem (always folly, ever enduring) of God or gods or the ground of Being, the big, even biggest questions, asked out of our need for answers by frail and failing souls.

PMcC: Thank you so very much for such an insightful, stimulating and enlightening interview, Peter.

Jennifer A McGowan

If you wish to become a poem

you must first dance with words.

The first dance may not be graceful.
This is all right. Practise.

When you hit puberty you will begin
to bleed stanzas. This is as it should be.

Teenage years teach you where your words belong,
which is to say, everywhere. Develop your voice.

You will need to learn and unlearn grammar,
so your words will punch. Or plead.

There are things in the world that will
knock words out of you. Keep loving them.

They will return. Put diction as your first priority.
Bow to rhythm, your partner. Find or discard

form. Alvin Ailey and Martha Graham were poems.
So was Balanchine. Never be afraid.

Start using nouns as accessories. Verbs
as shoes. Modifiers as daily dress.

Write *everything*. Learn to be fierce.
The world will make you angry. Rewrite it.

When your eyes open, you will have become a poem.

Biographies

Elizabeth Barton read English at Christ's College, Cambridge, after which she worked as a teacher. She has lived in Spain and the U.S. and now lives in Surrey where she is Stanza Rep for Mole Valley Poets. Her poems have appeared in magazines including *Agenda, Acumen, Orbis, South, The Curlew* and *The Frogmore Papers*. This year, one of her poems was shortlisted for the Enfield Poets' Poetry Competition and another was commended in the Poetry Society's Stanza Poetry Competition.

William Bedford's poetry has appeared *Agenda, Encounter, The John Clare Society Journal, London Magazine, The New Statesman, Poetry Review, The Tablet, The Washington Times* and many others. Red Squirrel Press published *The Fen Dancing* in March 2014 and *The Bread Horse* in October 2015. He won first prize in the 2014 *London Magazine* International Poetry Competition. Dempsey & Windle published *Chagall's Circus* in April 2019. His latest collection, *The Dancers of Colbek*, was published by Two Rivers Press in January 2020.

Liz Byrne was born and grew up in Dublin. She now lives on the edge of the West Pennine Moors. She worked in the NHS as a clinical psychologist until her retirement. She was shortlisted for the Bridport Poetry Prize, 2019, has had poems commended in the Open Space Poetry Competition and was a finalist in the Borderlines Poetry Competition, 2017. Her poetry appears in *The Curlew, Obsessed with Pipework, Orbis, Agenda* online and *Butcher's Dog*.

Hélène Cardona's recent books include *Life in Suspension* and *Dreaming My Animal Selves* (Salmon Poetry) and the translations *Birnam Wood* (José Manuel Cardona, Salmon Poetry), *Beyond Elsewhere* (Gabriel Arnou-Laujeac, White Pine Press), *Ce que nous portons* (Dorianne Laux, Éditions du Cygne), and Walt Whitman's *Civil War Writings* for WhitmanWeb. Her work has been translated into 16 languages. The recipient of over 20 honours & awards, she holds an MA in American Literature from the Sorbonne, worked as a translator for the Canadian Embassy, and taught at Hamilton College and Loyola Marymount University.

Dylan Carpenter lives in Santiago de Compostela, Spain. His poetry appears in *Cimarron Review, The Hopkins Review, The Iowa Review, Poetry Northwest*, and other journals.

Belinda Cooke completed her PhD on Robert Lowell's interest in Osip Mandelstam in 1993. Her books to date are: *Resting Place* (Flarestack Publishing, 2008); *Paths of the Beggarwoman: Selected Poems of Marina Tsvetaeva*, (Worple Press, 2008). *Flags* by Boris Poplavsky, in collaboration with Richard McKane (Shearsman Press, 2009); the Kazakh epic *Kulgaer* by Ilias Jansugurov (Kazakh NTA, 2017) *Forms of Exile:Selected Poems of Marina Tsvetaeva* (the High Window Press, 2019); (et al) Contemporary Kazakh Poetry (C U.P, 2019); *Stem* (The High Window, 2020) and *Days of the Shorthanded Shovelists* (forthcoming, Salmon Poetry). She currently lives on the west coast of Scotland.

D. V. Cooke (David Vincent Cooke) was born in Cheshire and graduated in English from London University. He worked for a number of years for *The Poetry Library* in London and has been published in numerous poetry magazines including: *Acumen, Babel, Envoi, Frogmore Papers, Orbis, Outposts, Poetry Wales, Stand, Swansea Review, Tandem* and *Agenda*.

Martyn Crucefix: recent publications are *Cargo of Limbs* (Hercules Editions, 2019), *These Numbered Days*, translations of the poems of Peter Huchel (Shearsman, 2019) and *The Lovely Disciplines* (Seren, 2017). Currently a Royal Literary Fund fellow at Westminster University, he blogs regularly on poetry, translation and teaching at www.martyncrucefix.com

John F. Deane was born on Achill Island off the west coast of Ireland. He is founder of Poetry Ireland, and its journal *The Poetry Ireland Review*. He has published many collections of poetry, including *Snow Falling on Chestnut Hill: New & Selected poems* (Carcanet 2012); most recently *Dear Pilgrims* (Carcanet 2018), and a 'poetry and faith memoir', *Give Dust a Tongue* (Columba Press 2015). A collection of poems set on Achill Island with paintings by John Behan, *Achill: The Island* published by Currach Press appeared in 2018. In 2016 Deane was the Teilhard de Chardin Fellow in Catholic Studies in Loyola University, Chicago and taught a course in poetry.

Terence Dooley's translation of Mariano Peyrou's *The Year of the Crab* was a Poetry Book Society Recommendation for Spring last year. His translation of Eduardo Moga's anthology *Streets where to walk is to embark: Spanish Poets in London* and of *(Sur)rendering* by Mario Martín Gijón came out earlier this year, also with Shearsman Books, and his *10 Spanish Contemporary Women Poets* has just been published. His own poems, *The Why of it*, are published by The Argent Press. He has a poem nominated for this year's Forward Prize.

John Greening (b.1954) is a Bridport Prize and Cholmondeley Award winner. He has published over twenty collections large and small, including *The Silence* (Carcanet, 2019), and has edited Grigson and Blunden along with several anthologies. This year sees publication of his edition of Iain Crichton Smith's poetry (Carcanet, November) and a major anthology of modern country house poems, *Hollow Palaces* (with Kevin Gardner, Liverpool UP). His collected essays and reviews, *Vapour Trails* (Shoestring) have just come out, along with a collaborative book of sonnets (with Stuart Henson) from Red Squirrel Press. www.johngreening.co.uk

James Harpur has published six books of poetry with Anvil Press and Carcanet. His latest book is *The White Silhouette*, an Irish Times Book of the Year. www.jamesharpur.com

Gill Learner's poetry has been published in a wide range of magazines including *Agenda*, *Acumen*, *The North* and *Poetry News*, and anthologies such as those from The Emma Press and Grey Hen Press. She has also won a number of prizes. Her first collection, *The Agister's Experiment*, appeared in 2011 and her second, *Chill Factor*, in 2016, both from Two Rivers Press. A third collection is in preparation for 2021.

John Robert Lee is a Saint Lucian writer. His *Collected Poems 1975-2015* was published by Peepal Tree in 2017. His new *Pierrot* is published by Peepal Tree, February 2020. His *Saint Lucian writers and writing: an author index*, a comprehensive bibliography of Saint Lucian literature (poetry, prose-fiction and non-fiction) was published by Papillote Press in 2019.

Jane Lovell is an award-winning poet whose work is steeped in natural history, science and folklore. A recent collection is *This Tilting Earth* published by Seren. Jane also writes for Dark Mountain and Elementum Journal. She is Writer-in-Residence at Rye Harbour Nature Reserve. Her collection, *The God of Lost Ways*, has just come out from Indigo Dreams.

Merryn MacCarthy lives in the Gers, France. She is a prize-winning poet, with two collections to her name, *Playing Truant* (Agenda Editions), and the bi-lingual collection, *Seeking the Mountains*: *À La Recherche des Montagnes*.

Of London-Welsh origins, **Sue Mackrell** has an MA (Distinction) in Creative Writing from Loughborough University and has taught in universities and FE colleges. She has worked on a range of Arts Council, Heritage England and Heritage Lottery funded projects, writing about those in history whose stories have been hidden or suppressed. As well as *Agenda*, her poetry has appeared in, amongst other publications, *Diversifly* (Fairacre Press,) online in *The Ekphrastic Review,* and in Leicester public toilets as part of the Everybody's Reading Festival.

Richie McCaffery lives in Alnwick, Northumberland. He is the author of two poetry collections from Nine Arches Press: *Cairn* (2014) and *Passport* (2018). In addition, he has also published three pamphlets including *Spinning Plates* (HappenStance Press, 2012) and *First Hare* (Mariscat Press, 2020). He is also the editor of *Sydney Goodsir Smith, Poet: Essays on his Life and Work* (Brill, 2020).

Gill McEvoy won the 2015 Michael Marks Award with *The First Telling* (Happenstance Press). Two collections from Cinnamon Press: *The Plucking Shed*, 2010 and *Rise*, 2013. 2012 Hawthornden Fellow. Gill lives in Devon where she is involved in planting wildflowers in her village.

Jennifer A. McGowan won the *Prole* pamphlet competition in 2020, and as a result, Prolebooks published her winning pamphlet, *Still Lives with Apocalypse*. She has been published in several countries, in journals such as *The Rialto, Pank, The Connecticut Review*, *Acumen* and of course *Agenda*. She is a disabled poet who has had Long Covid for seven months at time of writing. 'Interesting times.' www.jenniferamcgowan.com

W S Milne is shielding due to Covid-19. He is writing an essay on the Scottish poet Edith Anne Robertson for *Lallans* magazine, and making notes for a longish poem. He has written several plays in Scots.

Jessica Mookherjee is a poet of Bengali origin. She grew up in Wales and London and now lives in Kent. She has been published in many print and online journals including *Agenda*, *Poetry Wales*, *The North*, *Rialto*, *Under the Radar*, *Birmingham Literary Review* and *The Moth*. Her pamphlets are *The Swell* (TellTale Press 2016) and *Joyride* (BLER Press 2017). Her poems appear in various anthologies including the forthcoming Bloodaxe's *Staying Human* and she was highly commended in the 2017 Forward Prize. Her first collection, *Flood*, was published by Cultured Llama in 2018 and her second, *Tigress*, by Nine Arches Press in 2019. She is a joint editor of Against the Grain Poetry Press.

Abegail Morley's fourth collection, *The Unmapped Woman*, was published by Nine Arches Press (2020). She is a Co-editor at Against the Grain Press and Editor of The Poetry Shed. Her debut collection was shortlisted for the Forward Prize.

Tim O'Leary's work has featured in many journals and anthologies. His pamphlet *Manganese Tears* was published by Poetry Salzburg in November 2018, and a full collection *The Unmaking* appeared in September 2019 from The High Window Press.

David Pollard has been a teacher and lecturer. His doctoral thesis was published as *The Poetry of Keats: Language and Experience* (Harvester and Barnes & Noble). He has also published *A KWIC Concordance to the Harvard Edition of Keats' Letters*, a novel, *Nietzsche's Footfalls* and five volumes of poetry, *patricides*, *Risk of Skin and Self-Portraits* and *Broken Voices* (all from Waterloo Press), *bedbound* (from Perdika Press), *Finis-terre* (from Agenda Editions) and *Three Artists* (from Lapwing Publications). He has translated from Gallego, French and German.

Elizabeth Ridout is a poet originally from Yorkshire based in London and Kent. Her poems and reviews have featured in magazines as varied as *Agenda*, *Use of English* and *The High Window*, and she has done readings and interviews at festivals and on BBC Radio. Her debut collection, *Summon*, has recently been released by Myriad Editions as part of their Spotlight Series.

Tony Roberts's fifth collection, *The Noir American & Other Poems*, was published in 2018. His second book of essays on poets, poetry and critics, *The Taste of My Mornings*, appeared in 2019. Both are from Shoestring Press.

Omar Sabbagh is a widely published poet, writer and critic. His latest poetry collection is *But It Was An Important Failure* (Cinnamon Press, 2020). He has published much short fiction, some of it prize-winning, and has two novellas: *Via Negativa: a parable of exile* (Liquorice Fish, 2016), and *Minutes from the Miracle City* (Fairlight Books, 2019). His latest publications are a single-author study: *Reading Fiona Sampson: A Study in Contemporary Poetry and Poetics* (Anthem Press, 2020), and a collection of previously published essays and articles on English literary subjects, classic and contemporary: *To My Mind or Kinbotes* (Whisk(e)y Tit, 2020). Currently, he teaches at the American University in Dubai (AUD), where he is Associate Professor of English.

Gerard Smyth is a poet, critic and journalist whose work has appeared in journals in Ireland, Britain and the United States as well as in translation since the 1960s. He has published ten collections, including *The Sundays of Eternity* (Dedalus Press, 2020), *A Song of Elsewhere* (Dedalus Press 2015), and *The Fullness of Time: New and Selected Poems* (Dedalus Press, 2010). He was the 2012 recipient of the Lawrence O'Shaughnessy Poetry Award from the University of St Thomas in Minnesota and is co-editor, with Pat Boran, of *If Ever You Go: A Map of Dublin in Poetry and Song* (Dedalus Press) which was Dublin's One City One Book in 2014. He is a member of Aosdána (Ireland's affiliation of artists).

Will Stone is a poet, essayist and literary translator. His first poetry collection *Glaciation* (Salt, 2007), won the international Glen Dimplex Award for poetry in 2008. His subsequent critically appraised collections *Drawing in Ash* (2011) and *The Sleepwalkers* (2016) are published by Shearsman Books. A fourth collection *The Slowing Ride* will appear in October 2020. Will's published translations include works by Gérard de Nerval, Emile Verhaeren, Georges Rodenbach, Stefan Zweig, Joseph Roth, Georg Trakl, Rainer Maria Rilke, Georg Simmel and Maurice Betz. Will has contributed essays, reviews, translations and poems to a range of publications, including *the TLS, Apollo, the Spectator, the London Magazine, RA Magazine, the White Review, Modern Poetry in Translation and Poetry Review*.

Anne Symons comes from Cornwall and studied at the University of Wales, Swansea. She has worked in the UK, Sri Lanka and India, teaching poetry and drama to deaf children and adults. Her work has been published in many journals. She is currently studying for an MA in Writing Poetry with Newcastle University and the Poetry School, London.

Marek Urbanowicz previously published in *Frogmore Papers*, *Agenda* and various anthologies. Awarded an MA in Voice Studies at Royal Central School of Speech and Drama in 2014. Part of the RADA Elders from 2016-18. Chairman of Poetry for Pleasure, a Brighton-based group that normally meets weekly to read poems out loud to a receptive audience. A qualified acupuncturist since 1979.

Influenced by his continuing studies of poetry, painting, film, music, and the Japanese traditions of Zen, calligraphy, karesansui, bonsai, ma, wabi-sabi, and mushin, **Nathan Wirth**, a self-learned photographer, has been trying – primarily through long exposure and infrared photography – to photograph silence. Anyone who is interested can see more of his work at: https://sliceofsilence.com/photography/